CONTENT

CW00546293

Library of Congress Cataloging-in-Publication Data

Names: Faltum, Andrew, 1947- author.
Title: Aircraft carrier Intrepid / Andrew Faltum.
Description: Annapolis : Naval Institute Press, 2022. | Series: Naval history special edition
Identifiers: LCCN 2021046300 | ISBN 9781682477403 (paperback)
Subjects: LCSH: Intrepid (Aircraft carrier)
Classification: LCC VA65.I57 F35 2022 | DDC 359.9/4350973--dc23
LC record available at https://lccn.loc.gov/2021046300

INTRODUCTION

THE U.S. NAVY'S FAST CARRIERS, WHICH WOULD BECOME THE centerpiece for American global naval power, evolved in the years following World War I as naval aviation developed in parallel. From the first carrier, *Langley* (CV-1), commissioned in 1922 as an experimental ship, through the *Lexington* (CV-2) and *Saratoga* (CV-3), converted from battle cruiser hulls, American carrier designs evolved from the *Ranger* (CV-4), the first U.S. carrier built from the keel up, through the

Burning of the Frigate Philadelphia *in the Harbor of Tripoli*, a painting by Edward Moran (1829–1901), is currently in the U.S. Naval Academy Museum Collection.

highly successful *Yorktown* (CV-5) class, which included her sister *Enterprise* (CV-6). The *Wasp* (CV-7), which had the same tonnage as the *Ranger* but with features of the *Yorktown* class, followed. A notable feature of the *Wasp* was the first use of a deck edge elevator on an American aircraft carrier.

In May 1938, an expansion program added 40,000 tons to previous treaty limits of 135,000 tons. This allowed for the construction of two 20,000-ton carriers, one becoming the *Hornet* (CV-8), built to a modified *Yorktown*-class design. The other carrier became the *Essex* (CV-9), leader of the largest single class of fleet carriers ever built. The *Intrepid* (CV-11) was the fourth ship in the U.S. Navy to bear the name, and she would serve for many years, becoming at one point the oldest active carrier in fleet service. Today, she lives on as the centerpiece of the Intrepid Sea, Air & Space Museum in New York City. This is her story.

Intrepid Predecessors

The aircraft carrier *Intrepid* was the fourth U.S. Navy ship to bear the name. The first *Intrepid* was a 60-foot bomb ketch of 64 tons, built in France in 1798 for Napoleon's Egyptian expedition. She was later sold to Tripoli, where she served as the *Mastico*. She was one of the Tripolitan vessels that captured the U.S. frigate *Philadelphia* on 31 October 1803 after she had run aground on an uncharted reef five miles east of Tripoli. The *Enterprise*, under the command of Lieutenant Stephen Decatur, captured the *Mastico* on 23 December 1803; she was taken as a prize and renamed the *Intrepid*. Meanwhile, the commander of the American squadron, Commodore Edward Preble, knowing that the *Philadelphia* anchored in Tripoli Harbor would become Tripoli's largest and most powerful corsair, decided to destroy the frigate before she could be used against his squadron. Decatur was ordered to prepare the *Intrepid* to slip into the harbor at night, board and burn the frigate, and escape to the *Siren*, which would wait just outside the harbor.

On the night of 16 February 1804, the *Intrepid* entered the harbor and two hours later was alongside *Philadelphia*. Leaving a small force on board the *Intrepid*, Decatur led 60 of his men to the deck of the frigate. After a brief struggle, without a shot being fired, the Americans took control of the vessel and set her ablaze, Decatur being the last man to leave the burning frigate. As shore batteries opened fire, the *Intrepid* made good her escape. When Admiral Lord Horatio Nelson, then blockading the French fleet at Toulon, heard of the *Intrepid*'s feat, he is said to have called it "the most bold and daring act of the age."

Months later the *Intrepid* was fitted out as a fire ship to be sent into the harbor and blown up amid the corsair fleet, but she exploded shortly after entering the harbor on 4 September and was lost with all hands.

The second *Intrepid* was a 170-foot experimental brig-rigged steam torpedo ram of 438 tons. Launched at the Boston Navy Yard on 5 March 1874, she left Boston in August and arrived at Newport, Rhode Island, before moving on to the New York Navy Yard. After a few months devoted to torpedo trials along the Atlantic coast, the *Intrepid* was decommissioned at the New York Navy Yard on 30 October. She was recommissioned on 28 August 1875, but, except for brief visits to New England ports in 1875 and 1876, she remained at the Navy Yard. She was decommissioned again on 22 August 1882 for conversion to a light-draft gunboat, but work was suspended in 1889, and she was sold to a private owner on 9 May 1892.

The third *Intrepid* was a 176-foot steel bark of 1,800 tons designed and built as a training vessel at the Mare Island Navy Yard. Armed with four six-pounder and two one-pounder cannon, she was launched on 8 October 1904 and assigned to the Yerba Buena Training Station, San Francisco, for duty until 28 February 1912, when she became the receiving ship there. On 25 January 1914, the *Intrepid* became receiving ship at Mare Island Navy Yard, where she decommissioned on 15 October. She was commissioned in ordinary at Mare Island Navy Yard on 11 November 1915 for use as a barracks for the men of the submarines of the Pacific Fleet. In 1920 she again became receiving ship at Mare Island. The third *Intrepid* was decommissioned on 30 August 1921 and sold on 20 December 1921.

THE BEGINNING

THE STORY OF THE *INTREPID* (CV-11) BEGAN WHEN SHE WAS ORDERED in May 1940 as a member of the *Essex* class. She would be among one of the most advanced class of warships of her day, with speed, armament, newer and more capable aircraft, and modern radars that spelled victory in the Pacific. Although the third ship of her class, her sisters the *Essex* (CV-9), *Yorktown* (CV-10), *Lexington* (CV-16), and *Bunker Hill* (CV-17)

Intrepid about to be christened at the Newport News Shipbuilding and Drydock Company, 26 April 1943.

UNITED STATES NAVAL INSTITUTE

all were commissioned before her. The *Intrepid*'s first significant milestone was when her keel was laid at the Newport News Shipbuilding and Drydock Company on 1 December 1941. America had not yet entered the war, but the urgent demand for aircraft carriers soon spurred the acceleration of her completion 17 months ahead of schedule. The second milestone was when she was christened during her launching on 23 April 1943. During the launching ceremony, it is Navy tradition that a woman sponsor christens the ship with a bottle of champagne or other spirits broken across the bow as the ship slides down the ways. The occasion also is a time for speeches by attending dignitaries expressing the hopes for the new ship's future career. In the urgency of wartime, those speeches often conveyed a sense of grim determination and national purpose. The *Intrepid* was sponsored by Helen S. Hoover, the wife of Vice Admiral John Hoover, who presented the ship with a mahogany-framed brass plaque with the inscription "To the USS *Intrepid*, success in battle and good luck, Mrs. John H. Hoover, Sponsor."

After launching, there was still much work to be done as a ship neared completion during fitting out. In the months before a ship was to be delivered to the Navy, the precommissioning crew (sailors who eventually would crew the ship) were selected and ordered to the ship. Sea trials, an intense series of tests to show that the performance of the ship met the Navy's requirements and to demonstrate that all of the equipment installed was functioning properly, were conducted and new construction ships also had to undergo builder's trials and acceptance trials prior to delivery, when the official custody of the ship was turned over from the shipyard to the Navy. At this point the crew began preparations for the third milestone, commissioning as a fighting ship on active service. While only a small group had reported aboard as part of the fitting-out detail, others were quartered ashore or attended specialized training elsewhere. Often, ships did not receive their final drafts of men until just before commissioning. Many of the skills needed were taught ashore at various schools and training centers, but experienced crew members were a precious commodity. Some of the wartime carriers put to sea with 70 percent of their enlisted and half of their officers without prior sea experience, many never having been on board an oceangoing vessel of any kind.

The commissioning ceremony marks the acceptance of a ship as an operating unit of the Navy, and with the hoisting of the ship's commissioning pennant, the ship comes alive as the crew ceremonially mans the ship. Thereafter the ship is officially referred to as a United States Ship (USS). Due to the press of wartime, the

Helen S. Hoover, the wife of Vice Admiral Hoover, christening *Intrepid*.

The mahogany framed brass plaque presented by Mrs. Hoover.

A broadside port view of the brand-new *Intrepid* at Newport News, 16 August 1943.

commissioning ceremonies themselves were often brief and businesslike. The *Intrepid* was commissioned on 16 August 1943 at the Portsmouth Naval Shipyard under the command of Captain Thomas L. "Tommy" Sprague. (Sprague had served in World War I and afterward was trained as a naval aviator. After serving as air officer on the *Saratoga* and executive officer of the *Ranger* on neutrality patrol, he helped commission the escort carrier *Charger* [AVG-30] and commanded her during her working-up period. After serving on staff duty he was selected to command the *Intrepid*. He later was promoted to rear admiral and went on to command a task group of escort carriers during the Battle of Leyte Gulf. He eventually retired as a vice admiral.) At her commissioning he told his crew, "Entrusted to us today is a fine ship. She has been honestly and skillfully built.

It is now up to us. There is much work ahead and there are many problems to solve before *Intrepid* will be ready. With your cooperation, loyalty, and attention to duty, we will get on with that job." He went on to add that "only in the cool courage and fearless bravery of the present crew, will the spirit of the heroic and undaunted crews of the past live again."

Commissioning, however, did not mean the *Intrepid* was ready for combat. After completing trials in Chesapeake Bay to ensure she was seaworthy and that any problems with equipment or construction defects had been corrected, Air Group 8 (CVG-8), under the command of Commander A. McB. Jackson, flew aboard on 7 October 1943. (Commander Jackson had made the first landing on the *Intrepid* on 16 September.) She then left for Trinidad and her final

F6F-3s of VF-8 on *Intrepid*'s flight deck while working up in the Gulf of Paria off Trinidad in the British West Indies, October 1943.

Intrepid off the east coast of Panama with Air Group 8 on board, 28 November 1943.

Overall Length:	870 feet
Beam:	93-foot hull; 123 feet extreme, gallery deck
Displacement:	30,800 tons; 36,380 tons full load
Flight Deck:	862 feet by 96 feet fore and aft; 109 feet amidships
Aircraft:	90
Armament:	12 5-inch/38 Mark 12 guns (8 in twin mounts, 4 in single mounts)
	40 40-mm Bofors guns in quadruple mounts
	55 20-mm guns

shakedown, the demanding process of working up for combat. Captain Sprague and the more experienced crew members began shaping up the green crew and air group through lectures and drills on such topics as fire control, damage control, material conditions, ballistics, general quarters, and launch and recovery of aircraft. From 12 to 17 October the *Intrepid* worked up in the Gulf of Paria, a sheltered expanse of deep water west of Trinidad, and then off Port of Spain until 27 October. Back at Hampton Roads on 1 November, Air Group 8 was detached while she conducted final checks and trial runs in Casco Bay off the coast of Rockland, Maine. On 3 December she departed with her air group for duty in the Pacific.

On 9 December, while transiting the Panama Canal from north to south, the *Intrepid* collided with the channel wall in the Gaillard Cut, which at that point is practically vertical and rocky. Captain Sprague requested a court of inquiry to determine the facts of the case, and the inquiry was convened by the commander of the Panama Sea Frontier. The *Intrepid* had proceeded through the Gatun Locks and across Gatun Lake without incident and entered the Gaillard Cut at about seven knots. As she moved out of a wider portion of the channel off La Pita, making slow left turns, she was caught in a shear that drove her to starboard into the channel wall. The inquiry noted that conditions in the canal often produce "back waves" that the Canal Zone pilot, who had the conn at the time, was unable to counteract by increasing left rudder, and stopping the left engines while increasing the right engines ahead two-thirds. When it became obvious that

Not all landings went smoothly during shakedown. Here a Hellcat from VF-8 has crashed into the barrier. Note the squadron and individual aircraft identification markings on the underside of the port wing.

a collision was about to occur, the starboard anchor was let go and both port and starboard engines were backed two-thirds. It was estimated that at the time of impact, *Intrepid* was making only about one and a half knots. When she arrived at Balboa, divers discovered that only one forward compartment had flooded, but

The *Essex* carriers were the last class to be able to transit the Panama Canal. Here *Intrepid* is proceeding through the locks with only inches to spare.

there were extensive dents on the starboard side and wrinkles caused by compression failure on the port side. The conclusion reached was that no blame could be assigned to the actions of either the pilot or the *Intrepid*'s crew. After temporary repairs to her stem, she proceeded to the San Francisco area, where her air group was offloaded to the Alameda Naval Air Station while she underwent repairs at the San Francisco Naval Shipyard at Hunters Point. She picked up her air group and departed for Pearl Harbor on 6 January 1944.

Arriving at Pearl Harbor four days later, Air Group 8 was detached and Air Group 6, previously assigned to the *Enterprise*, reported aboard. Air Group 6 was commanded by Commander Henry L. "Hank" Miller, who as a lieutenant had taught the B-25 Mitchell bomber crews of the Doolittle Tokyo raid how to take off from the carrier *Hornet*. The *Intrepid* would begin her wartime career as part of Vice Admiral Raymond Spruance's Fifth Fleet. Spruance, who had commanded at the June 1942 Midway victory, was a cool, calculating professional known for meticulous planning and the careful weighing of risks. Under Spruance was Rear Admiral Marc A. "Pete" Mitscher who, as commander of Task Force 58, led the fast carrier forces in the drive across the Central Pacific. Quiet and soft-spoken, Mitscher was a leader's leader who held the respect of all his carrier group commanders. He gave them their heads if they performed. "I tell them what I want done, not how," he said.

In company with the carriers *Cabot* (CVL-28) and *Essex*, the *Intrepid* departed Pearl Harbor on 16 January under Rear Admiral Alfred E. Montgomery's Task Group 58.2 to raid islands at Kwajalein Atoll in the Marshall Islands. (Another veteran of World War I, Montgomery initially served in submarines until switching to Naval Aviation in 1922, eventually being promoted to rear admiral in May 1942. He became commander of Carrier Division 12 in August 1943, flying his flag from the *Essex*.)

Intrepid with her bow aground on the channel wall in the Gaillard Cut, 9 December 1943.

ANATOMY OF A WARSHIP

UNTIL THE LATE 1930S AMERICAN AIRCRAFT CARRIERS WERE SUBJECT TO limitations imposed by various naval treaties. The *Essex* class was developed from the earlier, treaty-bound *Yorktown* class. Although designed after the lifting of treaty limitations, the *Essex* class was a halfway design that started where the *Hornet* left off. The *Essex* design was more than 60 feet longer, nearly ten feet wider in beam, and more than a third heavier. The flight deck was longer and wider (850 by 80 feet) and unlike previous designs had a rectangular outline. The flight deck was served by three elevators,

with the number 2 elevator being a deck edge type amidships on the port side. This deck edge elevator could be folded up for passage through the Panama Canal. A unique feature of the after elevator, which was offset to starboard of the centerline, was a half platform below the main elevator. When the elevator was in the up position, this half platform was raised to the level of the hangar deck, allowing aircraft to be moved past the elevator pit. Equipped with two flush-deck catapults, a third double-action type was installed athwartships on the hangar deck. (This hangar deck catapult was only installed on a few early ships and was later removed.)

Survivability was increased with a triple bottom hull for protection against magnetic mines, an effective side protection system with a 4-inch armor belt, increased subdivision of compartments, an armored hangar deck, and a split power plant (which could survive the effects of one hit). The geared turbine power plant was based on that developed for the *Atlanta*-class light antiaircraft cruisers. Two of the 75,000 SHP plants were paired for a total of 150,000 SHP. This arrangement had the most efficient use of space and also the best watertight subdivision.

These features, plus more antiaircraft guns, added to their survivability. Four twin 5-inch gun mounts (two mounts forward of the island and two aft) complemented the four port side gallery deck level guns (two forward and two aft), allowing the firing of eight weapons on either beam. There were two Mark 37 gun directors, one at each end of the island, to control the 5-inch guns. The 5-inch guns were considered effective against level and torpedo bombers, but automatic weapons in the form of Bofors 40-mm and Oerlikon 20-mm machine cannons could best counter dive-bombing aircraft. The numbers of these automatic weapons increased as the war went on.

The *Essex* class was the largest single class of capital warships in the 20th century. Of the 32 ships originally ordered, 24 were completed, six were canceled as World War II wound down, and two were scrapped after being laid down. These were either of the original "short hull" design or the modified "long hull" design. None of the class that had served in the war were sunk, although several were seriously damaged, and the remaining ships of the class continued to serve well into the 1960s and 1970s. The *Lexington* (CV-16), last of her class, served as a training carrier until 1978. The *Intrepid*, along with her sisters *Lexington*, *Yorktown*, and *Hornet* (CV-12), now serves as a museum.

5-inch Guns

In the 1930s the Navy introduced the 5"/38, one of the best naval weapons of World War II. (In naval parlance the 5" refers to the diameter of the bore while the 38 refers to the number of calibers, that is, the barrel length is 38 times 5 or 190 inches.) This weapon saw service on destroyers, cruisers, battleships, and aircraft carriers, as well as many other smaller vessels. These power-operated, dual-purpose (DP) guns were effective against both air and surface targets because they could be elevated to 85 degrees and had on-mount antiaircraft (AA) shell fuze setters. They fired semi-fixed ammunition, that is, the projectile and propellant cartridge were separate. Although hand-loaded, they were power-rammed, giving them a high rate of fire, and they could be easily loaded at any angle of elevation—highly desirable qualities for an antiaircraft weapon. The gun assembly itself was the Mark 12 and was used in a variety of mounts, which had their own designations. The normal rate of fire per gun was 15 rounds per minute, but a well-trained gun crew could fire up to 22 rounds per minute for short periods. The maximum range for surface targets was 18,000 yards and the maximum ceiling for engaging aircraft targets was 37,000 feet. Beginning in 1943 the proximity fuze, the most important antiaircraft development of World War II, made the 5-inch gun an effective weapon against aircraft.

(top) A close-up view of the *Intrepid*'s Mark 32 twin 5-inch mounts forward of the island. On the starboard side were four single Mark 24 open mounts on sponsons; two forward and two aft.

(bottom) The *Intrepid* retained single Mark 24 5-inch mounts well into her career, as seen here in 1967.

UNITED STATES NAVAL INSTITUTE

40-mm Guns

The 40-mm Bofors was a Swedish design produced under license and used extensively as an antiaircraft weapon during World War II. It was essentially redesigned for mass production and the naval versions were power operated and water-cooled instead of the manually operated air-cooled single barrel "army" versions used on many smaller combatants. The rate of fire was 160 rounds per minute per barrel, with an effective range of 2,500 yards (maximum up to about 11,000 yards) and an antiaircraft ceiling of over 22,000 feet. Each barrel was hand fed with clips of four rounds each. From 1943 on, the Mark 51 director, essentially a manually operated Mark 14 gunsight on a pedestal mount, provided fire control for the Bofors. The Mark 51 directors were located as close as possible to the 40-mm guns they controlled. They could also act as directors for the 5-inch weapons. The *Intrepid* was commissioned with ten quad 40-mm mounts—two forward on the island and two aft, one on the bow, one on the stern, two on the starboard side aft at the hangar deck level, and one each on the port side adjacent to the open-mount 5-inch guns. At war's end she had seventeen mounts, the maximum number for short hull *Essex*-class ships.

Quad 40-mm mounts in action on *Intrepid*.

20-mm gun crews on board *Intrepid* during operations off the Philippines, November 1944.

20-mm Guns

The 20-mm Oerlikon machine cannon was a Swiss design also produced under license in large numbers. Mounted singly on a simple pedestal mount with a 60-round drum magazine, it was aimed manually and could fire at a rate of 450 rounds per minute out to a maximum effective range of 1,000 yards. Since it operated on a simple blow-back principal (similar to many submachine gun infantry weapons) and did not require any electrical or hydraulic power, it could be put into action quickly. Using explosive projectiles, which were more effective than the older .50-caliber machine gun rounds, it was valued as a close-in weapon against attacking aircraft that had made it through all the other defenses. The early models used ring and bead sights but later versions were equipped with the Mark 14 lead-computing gyroscopic sight. The prestige it enjoyed early in the war was largely the result of its success in British use. Later in the war it proved ineffective against kamikaze attacks and began to be replaced by twin mount versions for more fire power.

Radar during World War II

Radar answered the problem of carrier fighter defense that existed before the war. Only radar could give sufficient warning and information to allow airborne or deck-launched fighters to intercept incoming enemy aircraft. The use of radar, however, also required some means of integrating its information with that from all other sources. The *Hornet* had a radar plot installed before the war to be "the brains of the organization which protects the fleet or ships from air attack." As radar came into general use after Pearl Harbor, the Navy gained experience in how to use it and interpret the information it provided. To make the best use of the information received from radar, radio, lookouts, or other sources, each ship had a Combat Information Center (CIC) to sort out and keep track of the

The *Intrepid*'s radar suite in November 1943. The SK air search radar is sponsored out from the starboard side of her stack, while the SC-2 is at the aft end of the platform atop the tripod mast and the SG surface search radar is atop a pole mast just forward of it. The antenna on the slender pole mast aft and above the SG radar is for the YE/ZB homing system. The SM fighter direction radar is at the forward end of the mast platform. (The Mark 37 fire control directors fore and aft have their associated FD Mark 4 fire control radars mounted atop them.)

situation for the commander. The CIC predated the *Essex*-class and early units had a small and cramped CIC in the island structure. Later, the CIC was relocated to the gallery deck just below the flight deck adjacent to the island.

As part of the last generation of warships designed without major design provision for radar, the *Essex*-class

ships were plagued with mutual interference problems and damage from stack gases. Space had to be found on the island for the antennas and as the number of radars increased, the island became more cluttered. At first the single tripod mast had an SK radar for long-range air search, an SG radar for surface search, and YE/ZB aircraft radio

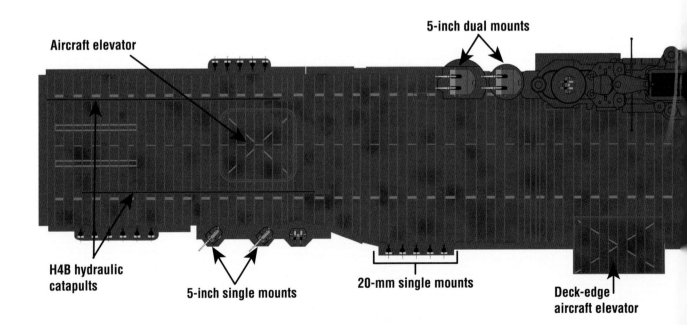

Aircraft elevator

5-inch dual mounts

H4B hydraulic catapults

5-inch single mounts

20-mm single mounts

Deck-edge aircraft elevator

homing antennas. The SK was probably the most important radar on the *Essex* class. Capable of detecting aircraft up to 100 miles away, it had a large 17-foot by 17-foot "mattress" antenna with IFF (Identification Friend or Foe) antennas attached to the top edge. With the addition of backup air search radars, a second mast was sponsored outboard of the funnel, usually a lattice mast with a smaller SC-2 air search radar. A second SG surface search radar added abaft the funnel made up for blind spots from the other radars. Accurate height finding was needed to control fighters efficiently and an SM height-finding radar was added, usually in the position atop the tripod mast previously occupied by the relocated large air search set. Only at the end of the war did a combined air search and height-finding radar, the SX, appear. The SX displaced the secondary air search set, allowing the antenna arrangement to be simplified. As commissioned *Intrepid* had her SK radar atop the mast, but in November 1943 it was moved to the starboard side of the stack and was moved again in June 1944 to a platform aft of the mast.

Catapults

The catapults for the *Essex* class were the hydraulic Type H Mark IV. The hangar deck catapult was designated H4A and the flight deck catapult H4B. Hydraulic catapults used a ram that drove a shuttle through a cable and sheave arrangement, which multiplied the speed and stroke of the ram mechanically. Pressurized air entered an accumulating tank, the pressure was transmitted to a piston inside a hydraulic cylinder by the hydraulic fluid, and the ram was driven by the piston. At the end of the catapult stroke, fluid was pumped to the other side of the piston, returning the catapult to the starting position.

Until World War II, the catapults installed in U.S. carriers did not achieve any great operational significance, partly because rolling takeoffs were both simpler and faster. Initially, rolling takeoffs presented no problems, but as aircraft loads increased and as air groups increased in size, less deck space was available. Typically, an entire deck-load strike would be spotted on the flight deck, leaving just enough room for catapult takeoffs. As soon as

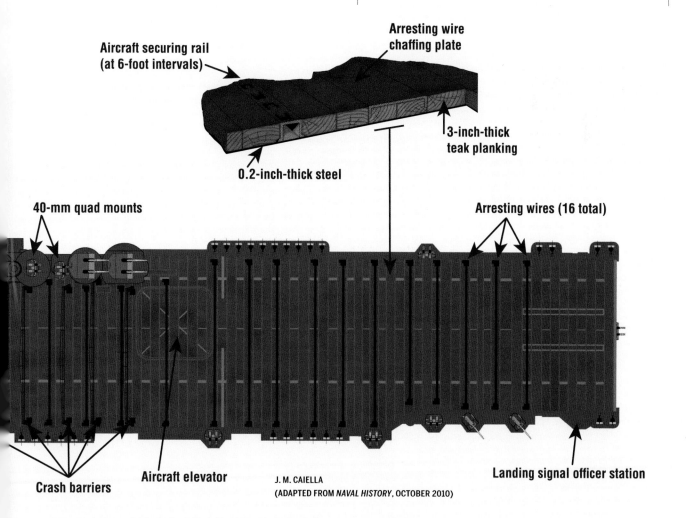

Aircraft securing rail (at 6-foot intervals)

Arresting wire chaffing plate

3-inch-thick teak planking

0.2-inch-thick steel

40-mm quad mounts

Arresting wires (16 total)

Crash barriers

Aircraft elevator

J. M. CAIELLA
(ADAPTED FROM *NAVAL HISTORY*, OCTOBER 2010)

Landing signal officer station

enough aircraft had launched, the rest reverted to rolling takeoffs. Since aircraft did not swerve on takeoff using catapults, they were safer at night and allowed launching without lights. Moreover, catapults permitted takeoffs in a crosswind, so that the carrier did not have to turn into the wind to launch. Catapults also offered flexibility in launching when the flight deck was damaged. By the end of World War II, some carriers were making 40 percent of their launches using catapults.

Before World War II the Navy stressed use of hangar deck catapults that could launch aircraft athwartships to provide an emergency capability to launch a scout aircraft if the flight deck was fouled or damaged, but the use of long-range search obviated this requirement. Also, the hangar deck catapults were not as useful in service as intended; air currents around the ship made launching aircraft tricky and they were seldom used. Only six ships—the *Yorktown*, *Intrepid*, *Hornet*, *Franklin*, *Bunker Hill*, and *Wasp*—were equipped with the sponsons, just aft of the forward elevator pit, with folding catapult track extensions for the hangar catapult, but *Intrepid* never had the catapult installed. Those ships that had hangar deck catapults had them removed later and a second flight deck catapult on the port side substituted. *Intrepid* received her second flight deck catapult during her yard period at Hunters Point from March to June 1944.

Arresting Gear

The arresting gear operated on principles similar to the catapults and had similar components. In the case of the arresting gear, the cable was run through a series of pulleys attached to the ram inside the hydraulic cylinder. A valve regulated the flow of hydraulic fluid from the cylinder into an accumulating tank. As the tail hook of a landing aircraft engaged an arresting wire (called a cross-deck pendant) stretched tautly across the flight deck, the arresting gear cable was run out, forcing the ram to compress the hydraulic fluid in the cylinder. As the fluid was forced out of the cylinder into the accumulating tank, the resistance provided by the valve had a braking effect, slowing the aircraft to a stop. The first wires had relatively soft arrestments since the arresting gear cables had longer run-outs, but those closer to the barriers had short run-outs and stopped aircraft abruptly within a short distance.

As the plane came to a stop, power off, the pilot raised his tail hook while crewmen came out from the edges of the deck to clear the wire from the hook. Just beyond the arresting wires were the Davis barriers, which were raised and lowered by operators standing in the catwalk at the edge of the flight deck. Once the aircraft landed, these operators lowered the barriers and the pilot could advance the throttle to taxi over them. The five Davis barriers just forward of the arresting gear wires were necessary because of the straight flight decks of World War II–era aircraft carriers. These barriers consisted of strands of cable that were at a height designed to snag the landing gear or propeller of any aircraft that failed to engage any of the 16 arresting gear pendants. (The barriers were also connected to the arresting gear engines.) The *Essex*-class carriers initially used improved versions, Mods (modifications) 5 and 6, of the Mark 4 hydraulic arresting gear used on the *Yorktown*-class carriers. One Mod had a longer run-out for the after section of the arresting gear area and the other had a shorter run-out for use closer to the barriers. Later carriers, beginning with the *Bennington*, used the improved Mark 5, which was fitted to all the *Essex* carriers after the war. Often in combat, however, even the Davis barriers could not prevent damaged aircraft from crashing into aircraft spotted on the forward flight deck.

ENTERING COMBAT

THE ISLAND GROUPS OF THE PACIFIC ARE ARRAYED IN THE FORM OF a capital "L." The Central Pacific Force would begin its drive westward in the Gilberts, an island group straddling the equator about 2,400 miles southwest of Hawaii. To the north and west are the Marshalls. Further west are the Carolines, strung out westward toward the Philippines. North of the central Carolines lie the Marianas, and above them, in a line aimed in the general direction of Japan, lie the Bonins. The forces of the Southwest Pacific Area under General Douglas MacArthur, moving along New Guinea's northern coast, complemented the Central Pacific drive and, occasionally, Central Pacific forces were called in

Intrepid in the Pacific with Air Group 6 on board, 26 January 1944. She was en route to launching strikes against the Marshalls as part of Task Force 58. Note the F4U-2 Corsair night fighter on the outrigger forward of the island.

to help MacArthur's forces. The Gilbert and Marshall islands, along with the Carolines and Marianas, are part of a group of coral atolls that make up Micronesia, which sprawls across the western Pacific between Hawaii and the Philippines. Kwajalein in the Marshalls, Truk in the Carolines, and Saipan in the Marianas were each a center of the overall Japanese defensive system. The closest of these was Kwajalein, the world's largest atoll. Operation Flintlock, the campaign against the Japanese in the Marshall Islands, involved the invasions

Strike photographs shot by TBF Avengers of VT-6 during attacks against Roi and Namur in the Marshalls, 2 February 1944.

of Kwajalein, Eniwetok, and Majuro atolls. On 29 January 1944 Task Force 58 launched strikes against the Marshalls. Task Group 58.1 hit Maloelap, Task Group 58.3 hit Kwajalein Island, Task Group 58.4 bombed Wotje, while Task Group 58.2 attacked the airfield on Roi. The *Intrepid*'s mission as part of Task Group 58.2 was to conduct air strikes against the islands of Roi and Namur before the landings and to provide air cover. At 0630 on the 29th the *Intrepid* launched its first strike against Roi and successive daylight strikes were launched against Roi and Namur until the afternoon of 1 February, by which time these islands had been secured and, since there was little airborne opposition,

the remainder of her air operations included combat air and antisubmarine patrols. (During the night of 29 January and into the following day, the battleships of the task group also conducted bombardments of Roi and Namur.) The few Japanese aircraft that were airborne over Roi had been shot down by Hellcats from the *Essex*, *Intrepid*, and *Cabot*, which then strafed parked aircraft on the airstrips. To ensure the Japanese did not stage through Eniwetok, Task Group 58.3 shifted to Eniwetok for the next three days, while Task Group 58.4 moved to Maloelap for two days and joined Task Group 58.3 at Eniwetok on the third day. While Task Group 58.2 was hitting Roi-Namur, Task Group 58.1 had been hitting Kwajalein, while land-based air worked over Mili and Jaluit. The fast carriers lost 17 fighters and five torpedo aircraft to enemy action, and 27 other aircraft operationally.

From 31 January to 3 February, the carrier aircraft took directions from the air support commanders in hitting Japanese defensive positions. After Kwajalein fell on 4 February, Task Groups 58.1, 58.2, and 58.3 headed for the newly occupied Majuro Atoll to refuel and re-arm while Task Group 58.4 continued strikes against Eniwetok. Majuro, 2,000 miles west of Pearl Harbor, allowed commercial tankers to bypass Hawaii, cutting down on transit times to the forward area while service squadrons provided logistic support for the operational forces. In her combat debut the *Intrepid* had launched 654 sorties and Air Group 6 had shot down seven enemy aircraft in the air and destroyed another sixteen on the ground. One Hellcat was forced down in the water after being damaged by antiaircraft fire and an Avenger photographic plane, also damaged by antiaircraft fire, was lost over the side after landing aboard. After refueling, rearming, and receiving replacement aircraft between 8 and 11 February, the *Intrepid* was again ready for action. The next objective was the capture of Eniwetok under Operation Catchpole scheduled for 17 February 1944. Four atolls where the Japanese had airbases—Jaluit, Mili, Maloelap, Wotje—and Nauru, too, were left to "wither on the vine" as the Central Pacific war moved on. They became practice targets for new carriers, or veterans

The Pacific 1944

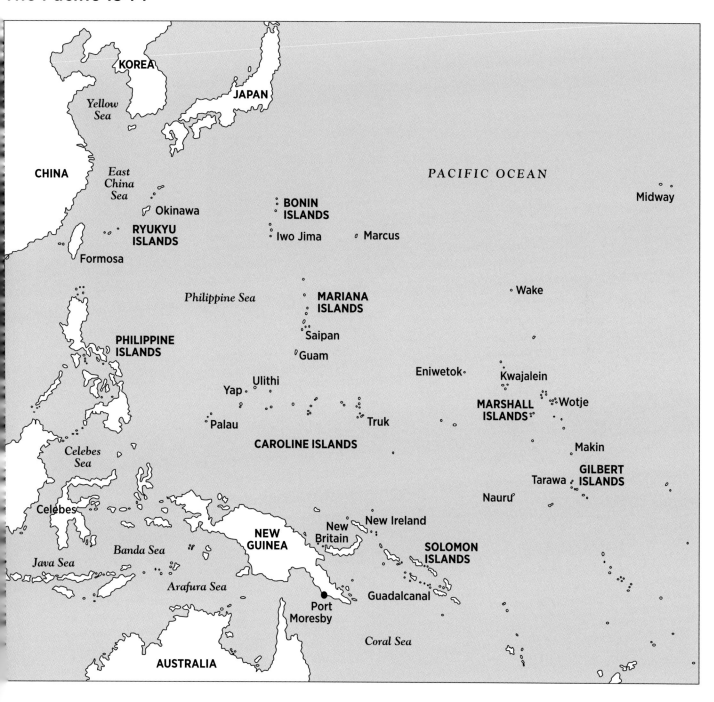

KOREA

JAPAN

Yellow
Sea

*East
China
Sea*

CHINA

PACIFIC OCEAN

Midway

Okinawa

**BONIN
ISLANDS**

**RYUKYU
ISLANDS**

Iwo Jima

Marcus

Formosa

Philippine Sea

**MARIANA
ISLANDS**

Wake

**PHILIPPINE
ISLANDS**

Saipan

Guam

Eniwetok

Kwajalein

Yap

Ulithi

**MARSHALL
ISLANDS**

Wotje

Palau

Truk

*Celebes
Sea*

CAROLINE ISLANDS

Makin

Celebes

**GILBERT
ISLANDS**

Tarawa

Nauru

New Ireland

New
Britain

**SOLOMON
ISLANDS**

Banda Sea

**NEW
GUINEA**

Java Sea

Arafura Sea

Guadalcanal

Port
Moresby

AUSTRALIA

Coral Sea

returning from overhaul, on their way to the forward area.

The next target for Task Force 58 was the fabled Japanese bastion of Truk, the "Gibraltar of the Pacific," located to the west of the Marshalls in the center of the Caroline Islands chain. Truk had long been held by the Japanese and threatened any future American moves in the Central Pacific; it would have to be neutralized for the invasion of Eniwetok and before the Marianas could be attacked. Task Force 58 sailed from the newly occupied anchorage at Majuro on 12 February 1944.

Captain Tommy Sprague on the bridge of *Intrepid* while at Majuro, 6 February 1944.

naval units of the Combined Fleet had departed on 10 February.

Some new tactics were employed for the Truk strike, including tighter task group formations and following under rain squalls on the way into the launch area. The first aircraft off would be a fighter sweep to clear the area of Japanese aircraft that might interfere with the bombers. Another tactic was to use 1,000-pound delayed action bombs on the last runway strikes to make repair during the night more difficult. Also, strikes against oil storage

Mitscher headed for Truk with three task groups, leaving Task Group 58.4 behind to cover the Eniwetok landings. When the aircrews heard that they were going to attack Truk, there were serious misgivings. Not much was really known about Truk and everything they had heard was bad. A land-based reconnaissance mission flown from the Solomon Islands on 3 February had shown some 20 naval vessels in Truk lagoon, but the major Japanese

sites were saved for last to keep the flame and smoke from obscuring other targets. The attack was launched at 0600 on 17 February when the task force was a hundred miles northeast of Truk. As the fighter sweep moved in, about 50 Japanese aircraft tangled with the 74 Hellcats of the fighter sweep. In half an hour, the Americans had dealt with most of the opposition, some of whom were tough veterans of previous battles. Within an hour and

a half, no more Japanese aircraft rose to challenge the attackers, and when the bombers arrived at 0930, there were no Japanese aircraft to interfere with their bombing runs. Some bombers carried fragmentation bombs in 100-pound clusters; others carried incendiary bombs and went after service installations on the airfields. Then came the dive bombers with 1,000-pound bombs, moving in to hit the shipping in the Dublon anchorage. Most of the Japanese warships had gone, but some merchantmen and a pair of cruisers remained. With the bombers came more fighters, who strafed antiaircraft positions that were firing at the strike aircraft.

The F4U-2 night fighters from VF(N)-101 Detachment B launching from *Intrepid* for the Truk strikes, February 1944.

As seen from an *Intrepid* aircraft, Japanese shipping is under attack in Truk Lagoon on the first day of raids, 17 February 1944. Four ships already have been hit. Dublon Island is at left, with Moen Island in the background.

The bombers attacked repeatedly, setting a tanker on fire, hitting a small carrier, and hitting the merchantman. In mid-afternoon a strike went after the other anchorages. A strike later in the day dropped the delayed action 1,000-pound bombs on the bomber airfield at Moen. A still later strike, almost at the end of the day, hit the revetments on the airfields, spoiling a potential night attack. The Japanese fighters reappeared later in the day, tangling with the strike aircraft. By the time the *Intrepid* retired that night her aircraft had flown 192 combat sorties, with VF-6 destroying 16 Japanese aircraft in the air and 37 on the ground as well as the damage done to shipping by VT-6 and VB-6. At the same time she put up eight combat air patrol and ten antisubmarine patrol sorties. Two cruisers and a destroyer were seen getting underway during one of the *Intrepid*'s strikes. One of the cruisers was hit by two torpedoes dropped by VT-6 Avengers and the same cruiser was hit by two 1,000-pound bombs dropped by the Dauntless dive bombers of VB-6, which also scored a hit on the destroyer with a 500-pound bomb. (All three ships were apparently sunk later by a battleship from the task force.) An ammunition ship was bombed by VT-6. The vessel exploded and the aircrew was lost when their Avenger crashed into the water near Eten. Another large cargo ship was attacked and sunk by VB-6. Six *Intrepid* aircraft had failed to return, one of which was flown by Lieutenant Commander John L. Phillips Jr., the air group

commander, but by the end of the day, large fires were burning on Dublon, Eten, and Moen.

Lieutenant Alexander Vraciu of VF-6 described some of the action that day in his report. "We noticed that the Jap pilots weren't reluctant to attack, but once they were cornered they'd dive steeply for the water or cloud cover. The Hellcat definitely can out-maneuver the Zero at speeds of 250 knots and better so we began to follow them down. I was able to follow three planes down in this manner, two being Zeros and one a Rufe [the floatplane version of the Zero], and set them afire. All hit the water inside Truk Atoll. While climbing back up for altitude after one of the above attacks, I noticed a Zero skirting a not-too-thick cloud so I made a pass at him, but he promptly headed for a thicker one, and after playing cat and mouse with him for some minutes I climbed into the sun and let him think I had retired. When I came down on him for the last time, from 5 o'clock above, he never knew what hit him, I'm sure. His wing tank and cockpit exploded."

The strikes on Truk had been a great success, reflected in the views of many in Task Force 58 that the Gibraltar of the Pacific had become the "Japanese Pearl Harbor," but the *Intrepid* was about to pay a price for her participation. Although she would be out of action for several months, the Truk strike had ensured that the Japanese would not interfere with the capture of Eniwetok, which later became a fleet anchorage.

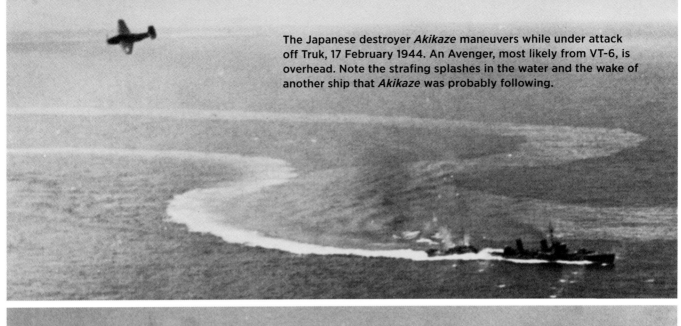

The Japanese destroyer *Akikaze* maneuvers while under attack off Truk, 17 February 1944. An Avenger, most likely from VT-6, is overhead. Note the strafing splashes in the water and the wake of another ship that *Akikaze* was probably following.

A Japanese ammunition ship explodes following a bombing attack by a VT-6 Avenger. The crew was lost in the explosion.

(right) Two Japanese ships being bombed during the attack on Truk.

(below) As seen from an *Intrepid* plane on the first day of strikes, 17 February 1944, the airfield on Eten Island burning at the left of the picture, while Dublon Island and town are in the middle background. Several merchant ships are offshore and one large tanker is tied to the fuel pier left of center.

UNITED STATES NAVAL INSTITUTE

Air Group

The basic unit of naval aviation is the squadron, and the number of aircraft and crews assigned vary with the type of aircraft and the current organizational doctrine. Early on, squadrons carried designations that reflected their missions. The "V" for heavier-than-air aircraft followed by another letter—"F" for fighting, "B" for bombing, "S" for scouting, "T" for torpedo—and a number for the individual squadron. Two or more squadrons assigned to a carrier formed the air group. Beginning in 1937, the term was associated with the name of the ship, for example "Saratoga Air Group." When the air group commander became an authorized command billet the following year, the air group became a formal unit. (Previously all squadrons were under the command of the captain of the

ship and the senior aviator in a given formation would be in tactical command.) At the start of the war a typical air group consisted of one fighter squadron with 18 Wildcats, one scouting and one bombing squadron each with 18 Dauntless dive bombers, and one torpedo squadron with 18 Devastators.

In 1942 carrier air groups began to be numbered and by the time the *Intrepid* was commissioned, a typical *Essex*-class carrier air group had a "double" fighter squadron of 36 F6F Hellcats, a bombing squadron with 36 SBD Dauntless dive bombers, and a torpedo squadron with 18 TBF Avengers. As the war progressed, the need for more fighters led to an increase in the size of the fighter squadron and, as the number of fighters increased, the bombing

squadron got smaller. The torpedo squadrons were equipped with the TBM, the version of the Avenger built by the Eastern Aircraft division of General Motors and the SB2C Helldiver eventually replaced the Dauntless. Beginning in January 1944 carrier air groups began receiving specially equipped and trained night fighter detachments flying modified Hellcats or Corsairs. Later in the war, fighter squadrons grew to the point where they were split in two, becoming fighter (VF) and fighter bomber (VBF) squadrons, though in practice they were interchangeable. Also, the F4U Corsair, which had problems operating from carriers earlier in the war began to equip carrier squadrons late in 1944 to help counter the growing kamikaze threat.

Hellcat

The Grumman F6F Hellcat succeeded the stubby little F4F Wildcat, the only Navy fighter that held its own against the superb Japanese Zero in the first year of Pacific combat. Looking like the Wildcat's younger but bigger brother, the Hellcat was unmistakably a product of the Grumman "iron works." It was chubby and angular, but rugged and powered by a magnificent engine, the

An F6F-3 of VF-6 landing on *Intrepid*, February 1944.

2,000 horsepower Pratt & Whitney R-2800 Double Wasp. With a wingspan of 42 feet 10 inches and a gross weight of nearly seven tons, the Hellcat was a lot of airplane, but steady as a rock when coming aboard a carrier. The Hellcat was the first Navy fighter designed on the basis of combat experience with the Zero, and matched or exceeded the Zero's performance in nearly every category except low-speed maneuverability. The

Hellcat's heavy armament of six .50-caliber machine guns could easily tear apart a Zero, and its self-sealing tanks, armor plate, and sturdy structure made it more survivable than its opposition. The confidence this airplane instilled in its pilots is best summed up in the words of Navy ace Alex Vraciu, who had served on the *Intrepid*: "These Grummans are beautiful airplanes. If they could cook, I'd marry one."

Dauntless

The Douglas SBD Dauntless was the Navy's workhorse in the Pacific and the deciding factor in the Battle of Midway, the turning point in the war against Japan. (It was the only aircraft to participate in all five engagements fought exclusively between carriers.) This two-place dive bomber was slow and vulnerable, but possessed long range, good handling characteristics, maneuverability, a potent bomb load, great diving characteristics, good defensive armament, and ruggedness and dependability that kept it in service long after its planned replacement by the Curtiss Helldiver. Considering its obsolescence, the Dauntless gave a good account of itself in tangles with Japanese fighters during the early part of the war, with its loss rate reportedly the lowest of any carrier aircraft. The SBD had a wingspan of 41 feet 6 inches and was the only carrier aircraft in an air group without folding wings. The most produced version of the Dauntless, the SBD-5, had two forward firing

Dauntless SBD showing bomb falling just after release.

.50-caliber machine guns in the nose and twin .30-caliber flexible machine guns for the gunner, who sat behind the pilot under the greenhouse canopy. Powered by a Wright R-1820-60 Cyclone of 1,200 horsepower, the Dauntless had a cruising speed of 185 miles per hour.

Avenger

Another Grumman product, the TBF Avenger was designed as a replacement for the aging TBD Devastator torpedo bomber and became operational just before the Hellcat. A large mid-wing airplane with a crew of three, the Avenger was powered by a 1,700 horsepower Wright R-2600 Cyclone and armed with one forward firing .30-caliber machine gun in the nose cowling, synchronized to fire through the propeller arc, one .50-caliber machine gun in a power-operated dorsal turret at the end of the long greenhouse canopy, and a flexible .30-caliber machine gun firing through a ventral tunnel aft of the large internal torpedo bay. Later versions of the Avenger had two forward firing .50-caliber machine guns. With a wingspan of 54 feet 2 inches, the wings had to be folded back hydraulically. Besides carrying torpedoes, the Avenger was used as a level bomber. It was a stable airplane but, although faster than its predecessor, was too slow and heavy on the controls to be used as a dive bomber. Production was turned over to General Motors' Eastern Aircraft division and GM-built Avengers were designated TBM. The Avenger was known affectionately by its crews as the "turkey."

A TBM from VT-18 in flight, August 1944.

Vraciu

Alexander Vraciu was born in East Chicago, Indiana, of Romanian immigrant parents. After graduating from DePauw University, he began his military career in 1941 and enlisted in the Navy. During World War II, he spent five months as wingman to Edward "Butch" O'Hare, the Navy's first ace of the war. During his time on the *Intrepid* Vraciu scored seven victories. His greatest success came during the "Marianas Turkey Shoot" while flying from the *Lexington* with VF-6, downing six Japanese aircraft in eight minutes. In December 1944 Vraciu's plane was shot down by antiaircraft fire during a mission over the Philippines. After spending five weeks with Filipino resistance fighters he returned to the *Lexington*. Vraciu spent the last few months of the war serving at the Naval Air Test Center in Patuxent, Maryland. He ended the war as the Navy's fourth leading ace with a total of 19 victories. After the war he was promoted to lieutenant commander and spent six years as a test pilot and was instrumental in establishing the postwar Naval and Marine Air Reserve programs. After serving in a variety of assignments he retired in 1963 as a commander.

Alex Vraciu poses on his Hellcat after the February 1944 Truk raid with his score as it stood while flying with VF-6. The Navy took a dim view of personal markings on its aircraft except for victory flags and small squadron insignia below the level of the cockpit rail, but unobtrusive names were sometimes tolerated, in this case "Gadget."

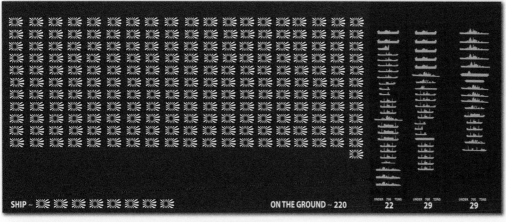

This "scoreboard" shows a running tally of the *Intrepid*'s victories painted on the ship's island. Japanese flags represented aircraft the carrier's planes and guns had shot down, and ship silhouettes were vessels her aircraft had sunk.

ILLUSTRATION BY KELLY OAKS (*NAVAL HISTORY*, OCTOBER 2010)

TORPEDOED OFF TRUK

THAT NIGHT THE JAPANESE WERE OUT LOOKING FOR THE TASK FORCE.
From around 2100 until midnight, small groups of bogies appeared on task force radars. The *Yorktown* launched a night fighter to drive off a bogie, but it had lost contact and was unable to regain it. The *Intrepid*'s combat information center still had the bogie on their radar screens and it was headed her way. Admiral Montgomery ordered emergency evasive action and turned the task group to a course of 240 degrees at 25 knots. When the contact was lost in the radar clutter from sea return, Montgomery ordered another emergency turn, but it was too late. At 0011 on 17 February, the *Intrepid* was struck by a torpedo in the starboard quarter just forward of the rudder. The ship lurched

In addition to the two SBDs on the flight deck thrown over the fantail, others were damaged by the shock, such as this VB-6 SBD with collapsed landing gear.

View of the starboard side aft where two after 20-mm gun mounts from Gun Tub 15 were carried away as well at the after starboard catwalk. The edge of the flight deck can be seen on the right side.

where all but two escorting destroyers were detached. Tommy Sprague was able to steer her by revving the port engine while idling the starboard screws. At first the passage was relatively uneventful, but the following day the *Intrepid* was ordered to proceed to Majuro and the change in course meant that the wind was now on the port bow and steering could no longer be maintained by using the engines alone and she became unmanageable. As Sprague recalled later, "She was like a giant pendulum, swinging back and forth. She had a tendency to weathercock into the wind . . . turning her bow towards Tokyo, but right then I wasn't interested in going in that direction." Wind resistance was created by spotting all aircraft forward and all cargo aft to keep the stern low in the water and the bow raised to provide more surface area. The outboard starboard shaft was locked while the port screws continued at full speed. This worked for a while, but when steering control was lost again 24 hours later a jury-rigged sail of cargo nets, hatch covers, canvas, and anything else available was rigged from the flight deck to the forecastle, taking some strain off the screws. Keeping anything like a straight course was out of the question, and the *Intrepid* made up her own zigzag pattern as she worked her way erratically back to Pearl Harbor where she arrived on 24 February.

violently to port and two SBDs on the flight deck were thrown over the fantail. Two after 20-mm gun mounts were carried away as well at the after starboard catwalk. Eleven crewmen were killed and 17 wounded. The *Intrepid* had been executing the port turn ordered by Montgomery when the torpedo hit and her rudder was stuck at 15 degrees left rudder. She continued her turn through the task group formation in a complete circle until she steadied on course 090 degrees. The detonation opened a hole from near the keel to above the fourth deck. The fourth deck in that area was completely missing and the third deck was pushed up to the overhead of the second deck, while fragments penetrated the hangar deck. What was left of the rudder was later described by Commander Phillip Reynolds, the damage control officer, as looking like a "huge potato chip."

Accompanied by the *Cabot* and other escorts, the *Intrepid* retired toward Eniwetok at 20 knots,

The makeshift sail on the forecastle, which helped *Intrepid* hold to a course, after a fashion, on her way back to Pearl Harbor.

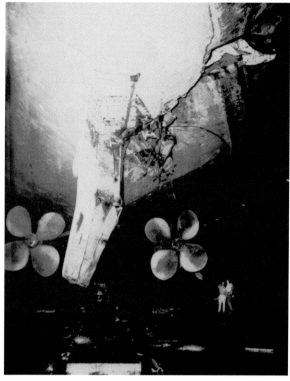

(clockwise from top) The damage to the hull structure is evident in this view as the water level drops while *Intrepid* was in drydock at Pearl Harbor.

The damage to *Intrepid*'s hull looking forward.

Intrepid's damaged rudder, the "huge potato chip."

Commander Reynolds thought that her makeshift sail "looked pretty rough" and wanted to remove it before the *Intrepid* entered Pearl Harbor but her skipper laughed and said, "Nothing doing." The *Intrepid* would become the only aircraft carrier to operate "under sail." In drydock temporary repairs were made. The hole was filled, but not made watertight, and the damaged rudder was removed in the mistaken idea that the *Intrepid* could steer by her engines alone. On the morning of 29 February, the drydock was flooded and with two destroyers as escort she headed out to sea where it was discovered that she was unmanageable. The *Intrepid* had to be helped back to Pearl Harbor but was unable to enter due to a storm. The only way to maintain control was to have the starboard screws going ahead standard while the port screws were two-thirds back, placing great strain on the engineering plant.

The *Intrepid* was finally towed into Pearl Harbor on 5 March by two tugs and entered drydock again where jury-rigged steering gear was attached. An auxiliary centerline fin, equal in area to the original rudder, was installed with a 100-square-foot section hinged at the after end to serve as a jury rudder. This jury rudder could be rotated about 20 degrees right or left and was controlled by wire cables passing through a pipe outside the hull and over sheaves at the deck edge on the fantail. The ends of these rudder cables were secured to tackle running to a capstan. The *Intrepid* put to sea again on 16 March and was able to make her way back to the West Coast where tugs helped her enter the drydock at the San Francisco Naval Shipyard at Hunters Point. Just before she pulled in, Air Group 6 departed to get back into the war on another carrier.

While still in drydock Tommy Sprague was promoted to Rear Admiral. His parting words to the crew reflected those at her commissioning. "Those of us who have served on this latest *Intrepid* have no apologies to offer to those gallant men who first established the name in the list of fighting naval ships. Brave officers and

The temporary hull patch can be seen just forward of the tackle for controlling the rudder.

men paid with their lives as did those on the first *Intrepid* for 'bold and daring acts' against the enemy. We too assaulted the enemy in his strongholds, severely wounded him and withdrew but to strike another day." The executive officer, Commander Richard K. Gaines, took over temporary command and would oversee repairs, while Captain William D. Sample assumed command for a brief period from April to May before being ordered to assume command of the *Lexington*, after which Commander Gaines took over again. On 30 May Captain Joseph F. Bolger assumed command and by 3 June the *Intrepid* was ready to rejoin the fleet. (Bolger was another veteran of World War I and an early naval aviator. He would go on to command the large carrier *Midway* [CV-41] after the war and eventually retire as a

vice admiral.) In addition to repairing torpedo damage, new 40mm quad mounts were added along with new fire control directors. She moored at Alameda where Air Group 8, spare aircraft, and miscellaneous cargo and passengers were loaded for transport to the Pacific.

On 10 June 1944, the *Intrepid* stood out to sea bound for Pearl Harbor. During the trip a casualty occurred to the reduction gears, requiring the number 2 engine to be secured and the number 2 propeller shaft locked. After she arrived at Pearl Harbor on 13 June, temporary repairs were made in drydock and she departed on 24 June for Eniwetok with Air Group 19 on board for transfer to the air station there. She catapulted the entire air group off while at anchor on 1 July and on the return trip transported casualties back to Pearl

Intrepid departing Hunters Point, 9 June 1944. She has her repairs and modifications and wears her new camouflage. It was common practice for carriers returning to the Pacific to transport aircraft and vehicles as deck cargo.

The hangar bay was also used for cargo as seen here on board *Intrepid* on her way to the Pacific, June 1944.

Harbor, her hangar bay having been converted to a temporary hospital. On 11 July the *Intrepid* was back at Pearl Harbor for 18 days of repair in drydock. On her first anniversary, 16 August 1944, her repairs completed and having prepared for her next combat tour, the *Intrepid* departed in company with the *Enterprise* and *Independence* for Eniwetok.

While underway, Air Group 18 under Commander William E. Ellis landed aboard and reported for duty. Ellis had picked up the nickname "El Gropo," which his men coined as a combination of his name, his position as group commander, his supposed shortcomings in navigation, and the fact that the large scale, multi-aircraft attack formations that were practiced were known as "group gropes." He would become air officer early in November 1944. Air Group 18 would soon engage in its first combat mission, and it quickly gained a reputation as a smoothly operating unit noted especially for its communications discipline in the air.

At this point in the war, Vice Admiral William F. Halsey was in command of the naval forces in the Central Pacific under the "two platoon" system in which the same forces were designated as the Third Fleet under Halsey and the Fifth Fleet when under

Spruance. Known as "Bill" to his friends and "Bull" to reporters, Halsey was the opposite of Ray Spruance. Where Spruance was cautious and methodical, Halsey was bold and brash. A latecomer to naval aviation, he earned his wings in 1934 at the age of 52. He was like a bull: he was the aggressive commander charging into the enemy like a raging bull, and also the "bull in the china shop" who could be his own worst enemy. Unlike Spruance, Halsey would be the real commander of the fast carriers and for many, the terms "Third Fleet" and "Task Force 38" were synonymous, often leaving Pete Mitscher, as commander of Task Force 38, out of the loop on critical decisions. While anchored at Eniwetok on 29 August, Halsey assumed command and the *Intrepid* became part of Rear Admiral Gerald F. Bogan's Task Group 38.2 and got underway for the Palau Islands. Bogan was another pioneering naval aviator who was promoted to rear admiral in 1944 after having commanded the *Saratoga* in late 1942. He served as commander of a group of escort carriers before becoming commander of Carrier Division 4 and Task Group 38.2. Although ambitious and often an outspoken critic of Halsey, Bogan was highly regarded by both his superiors and subordinates.

PHILIPPINES STRIKES

ON 29 AUGUST TASK FORCE 38 DEPARTED ENIWETOK. REAR ADMIRAL
Ralph E. Davison's Task Group 38.4, with the *Franklin*, *Enterprise*, and *San Jacinto*, hit Iwo and Chichi Jima in the Bonins 31 August– 2 September before moving on to hit Yap in the western Carolines on 6 September. Meanwhile, the other three task groups, Vice Admiral John S. "Slew" McCain's Task Group 38.1 with the *Hornet*, *Wasp*, *Belleau Wood*, and *Cowpens*; Rear Admiral Frederick C. "Ted" Sherman's Task Group 38.3 with the *Essex*, *Lexington*, *Princeton*, and *Langley*; and Bogan's Task Group 38.2 with the *Intrepid*, *Bunker Hill*, *Cabot*, and *Independence* would hit the Palaus 6–8 September. (McCain was in a "makee learn" status as a task group commander. He would eventually

A Hellcat from VF-18 launches from the starboard catapult. Note the light carrier in the foreground.

take over from Mitscher as the fast carrier task force commander.) On 9 September, Task Group 38.4 refueled and assumed a supporting role until the 18th, while the others hit Mindanao on the 9th and 10th. The task force encountered almost no enemy resistance and went on to hit the Visayas in the central Philippines 12–13 September, destroying almost 200 enemy aircraft and many ground targets and ships. Mindanao and the Visayas were hit again on the 14th, and Manila and the Visayas on 21, 22, and 24 September for a total of 893 enemy aircraft destroyed and 67 ships sunk. Based on the apparent weakness of Japanese defenses, Halsey recommended that MacArthur's Mindanao landings scheduled for 15 September be canceled in favor of immediate landings on Leyte. His recommendations were passed up the chain.

On board the *Intrepid* spirits were high as she approached her third combat operation. Her planes struck at Palau airfields and facilities on 6th and 7th of September, neutralizing potential opposition before moving on to Mindanao the following evening. The *Intrepid* launched attacks on Mindanao on the 9th and 10th, and her planes destroyed a number of aircraft on the ground at Davao Gulf and Matina. These strikes followed the usual cycle of a high-speed run toward the target and retirement afterward to refuel before the next series of strikes. It was

A flight of Avengers from VT-18.

during an evolution that one of her combat air patrols spotted a small boat filled with Japanese. The *Intrepid* had them picked up and turned over to higher command for interrogation. The *Intrepid* participated in the strikes against the Visayas from the 12th to 14th, after which she returned to the Palaus to support the Marines in their struggle against Japanese defenders in the caves on Peleliu on the 17th. As opposition was gradually overcome, the *Intrepid* resumed strikes throughout the Philippines and hit Okinawa and Formosa, neutralizing Japanese air threats to the upcoming landings on Leyte.

From the 21st through the 22nd, strikes were flown against Luzon followed on the 24th by strikes to the Visayas and a shipping strike to Coron Island. On 28 September the *Intrepid* and her task group anchored at Saipan for replenishment and rearming; they departed for Ulithi the next day. When the task group arrived on 1 October, Bogan shifted his flag to the *Intrepid* and, after putting to sea for a few days to avoid a typhoon, returned briefly before departing on her next combat mission.

On 7 October, Task Force 38 rendezvoused 375 miles west of the Marianas to begin a series of pre-landing attacks on Japanese airfields. The first task was to neutralize Japanese air strength north of the Philippines, primarily at Kyushu, Okinawa, and Formosa, then to shift southward to hit the Luzon and Visayan airfields. Despite poor visibility caused by overcast skies, Task Force 38 successfully attacked Okinawa shipping and airfields on 10 October, sinking 19 small warships and destroying over 100 enemy aircraft, for a loss of 21 carrier aircraft. Most of the crews were picked up by the lifeguard submarine. The next day, a less successful strike was launched against Aparri at the northern end of Luzon. On the 12th, Halsey began a three-day series of heavy air attacks on Formosa.

The carriers of Task Force 38 arrived at their launch positions before dawn. At 0544 the first strike, a fighter sweep to clear the air over Formosa and the Pescadores, was launched. In perfect flying weather, no fewer than 1,378 sorties were flown from all four carrier groups on the first day, followed by 934 the next morning. On the afternoon of the 13th, the Japanese struck back, hitting the *Franklin* and the heavy cruiser *Canberra*. On the third day the task force launched only 146 sorties, but B-29s from the 20th Air Force's XX Bomber Command based in China took up the slack. Japanese counterattacks crippled the light cruiser *Houston*, which was taken under tow. For a time, the air battle was titanic, and Halsey's fliers turned in results that rivaled those of the "Great Marianas Turkey Shoot" during the battle of the Philippine Sea in June. On the first day 101 Japanese aircraft sorties, combined with intense antiaircraft fire, brought down 48 carrier aircraft, but at tremendous loss to themselves in aircraft destroyed both in the air and on the ground. Overly optimistic reports by inexperienced Japanese pilots, however, led the Japanese to commit their land-based aircraft to the destruction of the American fleet at this seemingly opportune time and place. Over 500 Japanese aircraft

The Philippines 1944

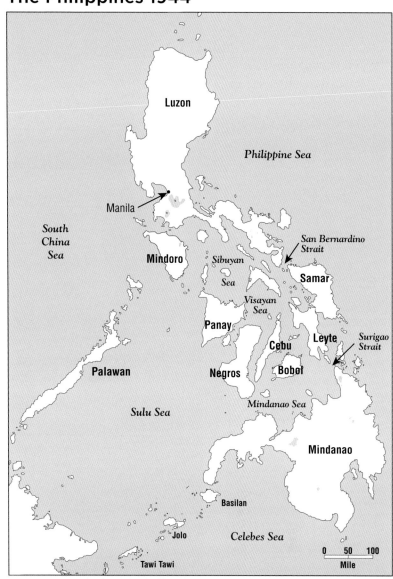

Four Japanese merchant ships under attack off the northern tip of Luzon during carrier strikes by Task Force 38, October 1944.

were destroyed along with some light shipping and installations. Japan had prematurely sacrificed its air strength for the defense of the Philippines.

With Formosa neutralized, Task Force 38 turned its attention to the isolation of the Leyte beachhead. On 15 October, Task Group 38.4 began five days of strikes against Luzon, and was joined by Task Group 38.1 and Task Group 38.2 on the 18th. On 15 October three enemy planes attacked the *Franklin*. One managed to get through and score a hit. The next day, the fast carriers paid their first visit to Manila. In anticipation of Japanese reaction to the landings on Leyte scheduled for 20 October, plans were made to rotate carrier groups through Ulithi for rest and replenishment.

The vanguard of the American invasion forces had been sighted off Suluan on 17 October and the Japanese planned an all-out response. A "northern force" of aircraft carriers under Vice Admiral Jisaburo Ozawa would be used as a sacrificial decoy to allow Vice Admiral Takeo Kurita's "center force" of battleships and cruisers from Singapore to attack and destroy the landing force off Leyte. Ozawa's carrier decoy force would have just enough aircraft to launch a shuttle strike to Luzon and convince

A Japanese two-funnel transport burning off the northern tip of Luzon, October 1944.

A dramatic view of Japanese shipping under attack as photographed from the back seat of a VB-18 Helldiver.

Halsey that this "northern force" was heading for Leyte. The real blow would come from Kurita's "center force" passing through the central Philippines via the Sibuyan Sea and the San Bernardino Strait to descend upon Leyte Gulf from the north and east of Samar Island. This force would include the super battleships *Yamato* and *Musashi*, two older battleships, six heavy cruisers, a light cruiser, and several destroyers. Another "southern force" of two old battleships, one heavy cruiser, and destroyers commanded by Vice Admiral Shoji Nishimura, would transit the Sulu and Mindanao Seas and approach the landing area from the south via the Surigao Strait. The "southern force" would be supported by Vice Admiral Kiyohide Shima and his three cruisers from Japan. In every respect, the plan was suicidal. The Imperial Japanese Navy was laying down its life as a blue water navy to protect the Philippine lifeline, now part of the interior defenses of Japan itself. As these plans were put into action, Vice Admiral Takijiro Onishi, commander of the land-based First Air Fleet in the Philippines, took desperate measures of his own. On 19 October, he activated the Kamikaze Corps of suicide planes.

An SB2C-3 from VB-18 prepares to come aboard *Intrepid*, August 1944.

Curtiss SB2C Helldiver

The Curtiss SB2C Helldiver was a mediocre dive bomber that never lived up to expectations. Its role was eventually supplanted by other types of aircraft, although many of its early faults were corrected in later versions. The Helldiver was a large aircraft whose wings and tail seemed inordinately large compared to its fuselage. Like the Avenger, the Helldiver was powered by the R-2600 Cyclone. It was armed with two 20mm cannons in the wings and twin .30-caliber machine guns for the gunner. The early Helldiver design exhibited poor stability and low-speed handling characteristics and later modifications included lengthening the fuselage and increasing the area of the tail surfaces to correct these problems. Besides being a difficult aircraft to operate from a carrier, the design of the dive flaps caused buffeting in a dive, degrading accuracy. All in all, the Helldiver performed no better than the SBD-5 except for a marginal increase in speed and a heavier forward firing armament. It was nicknamed "the beast" by its crews, a title it fully deserved. VB-8 flew the SB2C-3 as part of Air Group 8, the *Intrepid*'s first air group, but when the ship arrived at Pearl Harbor, Air Group 6 came aboard with the SBD Dauntless and the Helldiver did not enter combat from the *Intrepid* until Air Group 18 began its tour in August 1944 with VB-18's SB2C-3s.

Aircraft Colors and Markings

After commissioning and during the period of her shakedown and deployment to the Pacific, the *Intrepid*'s Hellcats, Helldivers, and Avengers of Air Group 8 sported identification markings similar to the prewar system, where the squadron number, followed by the mission letter (F for fighter, B for bomber, or T for torpedo), and individual aircraft number were displayed in large white block letters on the side of the fuselage ahead of the national insignia. The aircraft were in the three-color camouflage pattern of Sea Blue upper surfaces, Intermediate Blue, and Insignia White under surfaces. (In 1944 fighters began to be painted in overall Dark Sea Blue, which was applied to other carrier-based aircraft soon afterward.)

When the *Intrepid* arrived in the Pacific and took on Air Group 6, which had recently been on board the *Enterprise*, large white individual aircraft numbers were displayed on the fuselage below the cockpit and, in the case of VF-6 at least, double-underlined in smaller size on the vertical tail.

In 1944 individual air groups adopted "G symbols," which identified the air group and were not necessarily associated with a particular carrier. In the *Intrepid*'s case, during her second wartime cruise from August to November, Air Group 18 was identified by a white cross on the tail with the individual aircraft number below it. In January 1945, a directive formalized the G symbols, which were now identified with a particular carrier. When the *Intrepid* deployed with Air Group 10 in February, the markings consisted of a vertical white stripe on the tail with a corresponding band on the right wingtip.

The final change occurred in July 1945, when letters were specified instead of geometric designs since they were more practical and simpler to describe over voice radio. Because the *Intrepid* was on her way back to the Pacific in August 1945, her aircraft were never marked according to the new system. The letter system continued through the postwar period and evolved into the two-letter system still in use, with the first letter "A" denoting units assigned to the Atlantic Fleet and "N" representing units of the Pacific Fleet.

Camouflage

The Navy's camouflage instructions during World War II called for different systems or "measures" to be used for ships operating under different conditions. The "dazzle" patterns so popular during much of the war were intended to confuse the enemy as to a ship's true course and speed and reflected concern about submarine attacks. Later in the war, as kamikazes became a threat, solid color schemes designed to reduce observation from the air became more predominant. It was not unusual for a given ship to be painted in several different schemes over the course of the war.

The *Intrepid* was commissioned in Measure 21, a "solid" measure where all vertical surfaces were painted Navy Blue (5-N, which had a reflectance of about 9 percent.) It offered the lowest visibility to aerial observers—day and night—and most early *Essex*-carriers were completed in Measure 21. While being refitted at Hunters Point in April 1944, the *Intrepid* was repainted in Measure 32/3A using Light Gray (5-L, 35 percent reflectance), Ocean Gray (5-O, 18 percent reflectance), and Dull Black (BK). This pattern had an identifying number, 32/3A, which included both the measure, which indicated the color range (32), and the design number (3A). The letter following the design number indicated the type of vessel the design was prepared for, in this case A for aircraft carrier. She carried Measure 32/3A from June to December 1944 when she was redone in Measure 12. Measure 12 was a graded system that provided moderately low visibility to aerial and surface observers in all types of weather. All vertical surfaces, from the boot topping to a line parallel to the waterline at the level of the hangar deck, were painted Navy Blue or Navy Gray (5-N). In 1945, with blue pigment in short supply, many ships were painted in Navy Gray (5-N), which had the same reflectance and designation as Navy Blue (5-N). Above this band, the rest of the vertical surfaces were painted Ocean Gray (5-H). Her flight deck had dull black numerals with white dash lines. The numerals and elevators were outlined in yellow and several fake yellow "X"s were painted off the elevators to confuse enemy pilots, which often used the vulnerable elevators as aiming points.

After the war, the Navy discarded camouflage patterns and adopted overall Haze Gray (5-H), which had a reflectance of 27 percent and was regarded as the best overall concealment under most conditions. All horizontal surfaces were painted Deck Blue (20-B) with 5 percent reflectance. The *Intrepid* carried these colors over the rest of her career, although her flight deck patterns would change over time.

Design 3A, which was also carried by the *Hancock* in Measure 32 and by the *Hornet* in Measure 33, which was a lighter system using Light Gray 5-L and Ocean Gray 5-O.

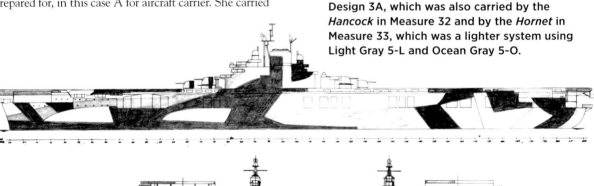

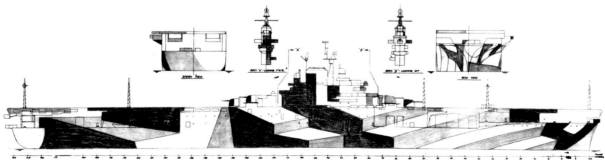

LEYTE GULF

AMERICAN OPERATIONS IN THE PHILIPPINE ISLANDS FELL UNDER the command of General Douglas MacArthur, who relied primarily on Lieutenant General George Kenney's land-based Army Air Forces for air support. "MacArthur's Navy," the light surface naval forces of the Seventh Fleet, was commanded by Vice Admiral Thomas C. Kinkaid. Halsey was to support the Leyte operation, but remained under the overall command of Admiral Nimitz and acted as a free agent as his Third Fleet commander. This divided command arrangement was the root cause of the problems at Leyte Gulf, especially in communications and coordination between the two fleets. Also, Halsey assumed virtual command of Vice Admiral Marc A. Mitscher's Task Force 38, leaving him a virtual spectator in the coming battles.

Intrepid photographed from the rear seat of a Helldiver, after taking off to attack the Japanese fleet in the Sibuyan Sea, 24 October 1944.

The Sixth Army landed on Leyte Island on 20 October under air cover provided by 18 escort carriers under the control of Rear Admiral Tommy Sprague, who had been the *Intrepid*'s first skipper. The escort carriers were organized into three task units known by their call sign, "Taffy." Taffy One was commanded directly by Tommy Sprague, Taffy Two by Rear Admiral Felix B. Stump, and Taffy Three by Rear Admiral Clifton A. F. "Ziggy" Sprague (no relation to Tommy Sprague). All four of the fast carrier task groups, joined by Fifth Air Force bombers, patrolled or attacked airfields. From the 20th through the 23rd, American aircraft met little resistance in the air and destroyed more than 100 enemy aircraft on the ground. The Sixth Army, moving steadily inland under this cover, hoped to gain as much ground as possible before the Japanese launched their expected air, naval, and ground counterattacks. For protection, Kinkaid counted on Rear Admiral Jesse B. Oldendorf's battle line of six old battleships, the escort carriers and their aircraft, and the aircraft of the fast carriers, which could range to 250 miles and still be within striking distance.

Halsey began to rotate his task groups to Ulithi for rest and replenishment, and Vice Admiral John S. "Slew" McCain's Task Group 38.1 with the *Wasp*, *Hornet*, *Hancock* (CV-19), *Monterey*, and *Cowpens* was 600 miles to the east when Halsey learned after daybreak on the 24th that two submarines had sighted Kurita's center force west of the Philippines in the Palawan passage. After carrier search planes had sighted both Kurita's center force and Nishimura's southern force, he ordered his three available task groups to cover the approaches to Leyte Gulf. Rear Admiral Frederick C. "Ted" Sherman's Task Group 38.3 with the *Essex*, *Lexington*, and *Princeton*; the *Langley* would cover the northern approach and was to stay off the Polillo Islands east of Luzon. Rear Admiral Gerald F. Bogan's weakened Task Group 38.2, with the *Intrepid*, *Cabot*, and the night carrier *Independence*, was off the San Bernardino Strait. Rear Admiral Ralph E. Davison's Task Group 38.4, with the *Franklin*, *Enterprise*, *San Jacinto*, and *Belleau Wood*, was to the south covering the Surigao Strait. Halsey recalled Task Group 38.1, arranging an at-sea refueling for the task group for the next morning. Halsey also ordered air strikes to begin, with Task Groups 38.3 and 38.4 to close on Task Group 38.2, the closest to the enemy.

During the morning all three task groups were heavily engaged. To the south Task Group 38.4 made ineffective attacks on the southern force, after which

The Japanese center force in the Tablas Strait before it entered the Sibuyan Sea, as photographed by an *Intrepid* plane during the Battle of Leyte Gulf, 24 October 1944.

UNITED STATES NAVAL INSTITUTE

it was ordered to assist Task Group 38.2, whose planes were attacking the center force in the Sibuyan Sea. Meanwhile, Sherman's Task Group 38.3 came under heavy air attack by Japanese aircraft from Luzon and he had to break off his air strikes and concentrate on defending his task group. Although over 50 Japanese aircraft were shot down or turned away, one got through to hit the light carrier *Princeton* (CVL-23) with a bomb that went through several decks before exploding. Her crew struggled to save their ship, but she was rocked by a tremendous explosion when torpedoes stowed below were set off. The cruiser *Birmingham* (CL-62), which came alongside to help fight fires, was also severely damaged by the explosion. The *Princeton* was abandoned and sunk later that day by a torpedo from the cruiser *Reno* (CL-96). She was the first carrier lost by the Fast Carrier Task Force.

While Task Group 38.3 continued to beat off fresh attacks, Halsey turned his full attention to the center force, concluding that Kinkaid could deal with the oncoming southern force, which would be within gun range of Oldendorf's old battleships around midnight. The battle in the Sibuyan Sea lasted from around 1030 to 1400. The striking aircraft met almost no air opposition, since Japanese commanders considered the attack on Sherman's task group to be more important than air cover for Kurita. On the morning of 24 October, while transiting the Sibuyan Sea, Kurita's ships were spotted by a reconnaissance aircraft from the *Intrepid*. About two hours later, the super battleship *Musashi* was attacked by eight Helldivers from VB-18 at 1027. One 500-pound bomb struck the top of forward turret but failed to penetrate. Minutes later, the *Musashi* was struck starboard amidships by a torpedo from an Avenger

(top) The Japanese battleship *Musashi* under attack by U.S. planes in the Sibuyan Sea, 24 October 1944.

(middle) The Japanese battleship *Nagato* and a *Nachi*-class cruiser under attack in the Sibuyan Sea, 24 October 1944, as photographed from the rear seat of a VB-18 Helldiver.

(bottom) The Japanese battleship *Yamato*, in the lower center, and other warships maneuver while under attack in the Sibuyan Sea, 24 October 1944. The shadow of one plane can be seen on a cloud in lower right center.

from VT-18. The ship began taking on water and listed to starboard, which was later reduced by counterflooding. Two Avengers were shot down during this attack. An hour and a half later, another eight Helldivers from VB-18 attacked again, one bomb hitting the upper deck, which failed to detonate, and another hitting the port side of the deck. This bomb penetrated two decks before exploding above one of the engine rooms, forcing its abandonment along with the adjacent boiler room. The *Musashi*'s speed dropped to 22 knots. Two Helldivers were shot down during this attack by antiaircraft fire. Minutes later, another nine Avengers attacked from both sides of the battleship, scoring three torpedo hits on the port side. One hit abreast the forward turret, the second flooded a hydraulic machinery room, and the third flooded another engine room. More counterflooding reduced the list to port, but the degree of flooding reduced the ship's forward freeboard. The 72,000-ton super battleship *Musashi*, having been repeatedly hit by bombs and torpedoes, fell behind, sinking. She retired and, later in the early evening, rolled over and sank. Kurita's other ships sustained damage as well, but he still had four battleships, six heavy cruisers, and other escort ships. At around 1400 he turned westward in apparent retreat.

The returning aviators were jubilant, and their exaggerated claims led Halsey to believe that the center force no longer represented a serious threat to the Leyte beachhead. Still, Halsey did not discount the possibility that the center force would turn eastward again, and he sent a preparatory battle plan to his task commanders to cover the possibility. Four of his six battleships, two heavy and three light cruisers, and 14 destroyers formed Task Force 34 under Vice Admiral Willis A. "Ching" Lee as Commander Battle Line. He later amended the plan by voice radio message to his subordinate commanders: "If the enemy sorties, TF 34 will be formed when directed by me." By accident, Kinkaid had received the first message, but had no way of intercepting the clarification message. He therefore assumed that the Task Force 34 battle line was formed and guarding the San Bernardino Strait. Admiral King in Washington and Nimitz at CincPac headquarters had also received the first message and assumed that Task Force 34 had been formed and was guarding the San Bernardino Strait.

With the Surigao and San Bernardino Straits supposedly covered, the next question on Halsey's mind was the location of the Japanese carriers. Sherman had permission from Mitscher to search to the northeast, and at 1405 launched a search in that direction. Ozawa, for his part, did everything he could think of to get noticed, including sending fake radio messages, sending out air searches, and launching a 76-plane strike against Sherman's task group. The strike was set upon by Sherman's Hellcats and the task group antiaircraft fire, but the Americans thought this was another land-based attack like the one that had bombed the *Princeton*. Sherman's searching Helldivers finally located the northern force at 1640, only 190 miles away. After weighing various factors with his advisors, Halsey reasoned that the center force might turn eastward again if he went north to get the Japanese carriers, but felt it unlikely that the center force would enter Leyte Gulf until late in the morning. He could run north to knock off the carriers, then turn south to help drive off Kurita. Besides, Oldendorf should have finished with the southern force by then and be available to assist if needed. Putting his finger on the plot of the northern force, he declared, "We will run north at top speed and put those carriers out for keeps." At 1950 he radioed Kinkaid at Leyte: "Central force heavily damaged according to strike reports. Am proceeding north with three groups to attack carrier forces at dawn." Sixteen minutes later, Halsey received a report from an *Independence* night Hellcat that the center force had been sighted in the Sibuyan Sea heading for the San Bernardino Strait at 12 knots.

This still did not stop Halsey. After passing on the contact report to Kinkaid, Halsey ordered Bogan's and Davison's task groups to join Sherman and ordered McCain to stop refueling and return. Kinkaid still thought Task Force 34 was guarding the San Bernardino Strait, but did not question that Halsey was leaving it apparently without air cover. Mitscher, also left in the dark, had assumed that the battle line would be formed when Task Force 38 headed north and did not learn that all the battleships were to accompany the carriers north until midnight, when all the task groups rendezvoused off Luzon. Both Commodore Arleigh Burke, Mitscher's chief of staff, and Commander Jimmy Flatley, his new operations officer, urged Mitscher to recommend to Halsey that he send the battleships back to the San Bernardino Strait with Bogan's task group to provide air support. Mitscher, still smarting from the rebuff given by Spruance at his suggestions off Saipan months before during the battle of the Philippine Sea, told Flatley: "If he wants my advice he'll ask for it." "Ching" Lee also told Halsey that the northern force was a decoy, but was ignored.

The run north was not really a run. As soon as Bogan and Davison, moving at 25 knots, had joined on Sherman, the task force slowed down to 16 knots. At midnight, Halsey turned over tactical command to Mitscher, who promptly increased the speed to 20 knots. Halsey ordered a 0100 night search from the *Independence*, despite Mitscher's protest that it would only alert the Japanese. At 0205, the radar-equipped Hellcats sighted Japanese ships only 80 miles north of the task force. That meant that a night surface action could take place around 0430. Halsey ordered

A Helldiver from the VB-18 "Sunday Punchers" is maneuvered into position on board *Intrepid* after returning from a combat mission with battle damage to its tail during the Leyte Gulf battle.

Lee to form the battle line and more time was lost as Lee slowly and carefully pulled his battleships out of the formation. Halsey again slowed down the task force when he learned that Oldendorf was engaging the southern force in the Surigao Strait. As it turned out, the Japanese ships only 80 miles away were the hermaphrodite battleships *Ise* and *Hyuga* under the command of Rear Admiral Chiaki Matsuda. Matsuda's battleships, which had flight decks installed on their after decks to operate floatplanes, formed the detached van of Ozawa's force. He was indeed seeking a night surface engagement to attract Halsey north. Ironically,

Matsuda, seeing lightning flashes to the south, mistook these for land-based air attacks on Halsey's forces. On the strength of Matsuda's erroneous report, Ozawa ordered the battleships to rejoin the carriers. When no surface battle materialized at 0430, Mitscher assumed incorrectly that the search aircraft had scared the Japanese off. He could only arm his bombers and launch long-range search-strikes at first light.

Meanwhile, Kinkaid was awaiting two-night battles. The one in the Surigao Strait began at 2230 on 24 October as PT boats engaged Nishimura's force and reached its peak around 0400 the next day, with the almost complete annihilation of Nishimura's ships by Oldendorf's battle line "capping the T." This was a classic surface engagement maneuver of the type studied by every battleship sailor since Japanese Admiral Togo used it to crush the Imperial Russian Navy at Tsushima Strait in 1905. Shima, following behind Nishimura, took one look at the destruction and wisely turned around. At the recommendation of Captain Dick Whitehead, the air-support coordinator assigned to Kinkaid on loan from the Central Pacific forces, the escort carriers prepared two fighter-torpedo strikes for the dawn mop up. One was for the Surigao Strait, the other for any stray ships that might have slipped past Lee's battle line in the expected second night battle, although Kinkaid had heard nothing further about the northern or center forces. PBY Catalina seaplanes would conduct night searches to the north.

As the southern force was being pounded to pieces, Kinkaid held a staff meeting to "check for errors of commission or of omission," but no one could think of anything. After the meeting adjourned around 0400, Kinkaid's operations officer, Captain Richard H. Cruzen, returned and said, "Admiral, I can think of only one other thing. We have never directly asked Halsey if Task Force 34 is guarding San Bernardino." Kinkaid agreed and at 0412 sent off a message to Halsey asking for confirmation of that fact. Halsey received the message at 0648 and replied in the negative at 0705, too late for Kinkaid to do anything about it. After the old battleships had mauled Nishimura's ships, Oldendorf had entered the Surigao Strait looking for cripples. By dawn, Oldendorf's battle force was 65 miles from the Leyte beachhead.

At daybreak on 25 October, the battle for Leyte Gulf was about to heat up. The PBY searches had turned up nothing of interest and the search flight for the northern sector was just being launched at 0645, when without any warning, the center force was sighted visually by the escort carriers off Samar. Within 15 minutes, 18.1-inch shells from the super battleship *Yamato* were dropping among the hapless escort carriers of Ziggy Sprague's Taffy Three. Taffy Three turned away from the advancing Japanese, laying smoke and calling for help. At 0707 Kinkaid radioed in plain language to Halsey that his ships were under heavy attack by major Japanese surface units. This message, like others in the divided communications setup, took over an hour to be delivered.

Mitscher had launched his searches north and then swung them eastward followed by deckload strikes. Ozawa was 190 miles northeast of Task Force 38 and steaming south when his radar picked up Mitscher's search aircraft. Ozawa turned away and managed to open the distance by another 40 miles before being spotted at 0710. The attack by Task Force 38 began with ten deckload strikes of Mitscher's orbiting planes, which had been waiting for the search aircraft to make

contact. First on the scene was Air Group 15 from the *Essex*, and Commander David McCampbell, the air group commander, became target coordinator. Ozawa launched his last 29 planes. The four Japanese carriers were sitting ducks. Unlike the hurried twilight attack of the battle of the Philippine Sea, the morning attack was well executed and systematic. The light carrier *Chitose* went down under a heavy bombing attack at 0937. A torpedo struck Ozawa's flagship, *Zuikaku*, forcing him to shift his flag to a cruiser. A second bombing strike set the *Chiyoda* afire, and she was eventually abandoned. Afternoon strikes by the *Lexington* and *Langley* finished off two of the carriers. The *Zuikaku*, veteran of the Pearl Harbor attack, was repeatedly bombed and torpedoed until she sank at 1414. The light carrier *Zuiho* was continually hit until she sank at 1526. Cruiser fire sank the abandoned *Chiyoda* at 1655. The old hermaphrodite battleships *Ise* and *Hyuga* managed to survive by skillful maneuvering and intense antiaircraft fire.

Meanwhile, the escort carriers battled for their lives and pleaded for help. Although Halsey had received Kinkaid's plea at 0822, he felt that Kinkaid could handle the situation with the forces at his disposal. As he stated later, "I figured that the 18 little carriers had enough planes to protect themselves until Oldendorf could bring up his heavy ships." The little carriers tried their best. Dick Whitehead recalled the strike planes going after the southern force cripples, and these attacked Kurita, but the other aircraft were

A Japanese carrier under attack by U.S. carrier planes off Cape Engano, 25 October 1944.

armed for combat air patrol, antisubmarine patrol, and ground-support operations. Without torpedoes and heavy bombs, these planes could only use what they had and many continued to make dummy runs to divert Japanese fire away from the escort carriers. The destroyers and destroyer escorts valiantly attacked the Japanese with torpedoes and 5-inch gunfire. Oldendorf was still three hours away and the Army bombers over the Visayas could not be contacted. Kinkaid and Ziggy Sprague pleaded by radio with Halsey to send the fast carriers and the fast battleships to save them from the continual pounding.

Halsey had all this information by 0930 but was not deterred. He did, however, order McCain's Task Group 83.1 to the rescue, although McCain's ships were over 300 miles from Leyte, a long flight for the carrier aircraft. Halsey needed several more hours to finish the northern force with his carriers and battleships. In desperation, Kinkaid called for Lee's Task Force 34 in plain language, but Halsey didn't turn around. Kinkaid realized at last that Task Force 34 was not guarding the San Bernardino Strait, but neither King in Washington nor Nimitz at CincPac headquarters knew its whereabouts. Nimitz fired off a coded message to Halsey asking for the location of Task Force 34. Not all of the normal cryptographer's "padding" was removed and Halsey received the message as: "From CincPac. Where is, rpt, where is TF 34. The world wonders." Kinkaid's communicators correctly removed the padding at both ends of the message, but Halsey's signalman did not, removing only the first phrase. Halsey received this message at 1000 and his first response was immediate. Losing his temper at this obvious criticism from Nimitz, he threw his cap to the deck and began swearing until he could be calmed down by his chief of staff, Captain Robert B. "Mick" Carney.

The Nimitz message prodded Halsey into action, but not before another hour had been lost while he thought things over. At 1055 he ordered the entire battle line south. Two battleships under Rear Admiral Oscar Badger and covered by Bogan's Task Group 38.2 were to charge ahead at 28 knots, but Bogan's destroyers first needed refueling. Halsey informed Nimitz of his decision: "Task Force 34 with me engaging carrier force. Am now proceeding with Task Group 38.2 and all fast BB to reinforce Kinkaid. . ." Halsey wanted all or nothing. He took all the battleships with him, leaving nothing behind to finish

off the *Ise* and *Hyuga*. By not dividing his battleships, Halsey allowed the *Ise* and *Hyuga* to escape, and by waiting until 1055 to turn south, he allowed Kurita to escape as well.

Although Ozawa had succeeded in luring Halsey away, Kurita did not capitalize on the opportunity. The fierce air and destroyer attacks had cost him three heavy cruisers, and at 0911 he ordered his ships to break off their pursuit of the escort carriers, intending to regroup his scattered forces before continuing into Leyte Gulf. He believed he had engaged and sunk several carriers from Task Force 38, although he had sunk one escort aircraft carrier, the *Gambier Bay* (CVE-73), and damaged others. After receiving a false contact report that had enemy carriers closing in from the sea, and fearing land-based American air strikes, Kurita decided at 1230 to clear Leyte Gulf. The action off Samar had ended. No American carriers appeared and Kurita, low on fuel, turned for the San Bernardino Strait and home. Just after 1300, as the center force retired, McCain's carriers attacked from far to the east, but did little damage. At around 2000 that night, Halsey ordered six night Avengers launched from the *Independence*. One of these spotted 15 ships passing along the coast off Samar and into the San Bernardino Strait. The night carrier men convinced Halsey to let them have a crack at Kurita, and Halsey agreed at 0300 on the 26th, but not before a severe thunderstorm had caused the aircraft shadowing the center force to lose contact. A strike of four night Avengers and five night Hellcats was launched, but did not locate Kurita. McCain and Bogan launched strikes over the Sibuyan Sea at dawn, with disappointing results: one light cruiser sunk and one heavy cruiser damaged.

The Americans had won the largest naval battle in history. Against American losses of the light carrier *Princeton*, two escort carriers, two destroyers, and one destroyer escort, the Japanese lost 45 percent of all ships engaged, a total of three battleships, one heavy carrier, three light carriers, six heavy cruisers, four light cruisers, and nine destroyers. After the battle, Kurita was blamed for his failure to complete the destruction of the American ships in Leyte Gulf, and was banished in December 1944 to the presidency of the Japanese Naval Academy. Ozawa became a hero for successfully completing his part in the battle and in May 1945 relieved Toyoda as commander of the Combined Fleet, although he was not promoted to full admiral.

THE KAMIKAZES

THE AMERICANS HAD WON THE LARGEST NAVAL BATTLE IN HISTORY, but the kamikazes had made their first organized attack on the American Navy during the battle, attacking several escort carriers on 25 October. The first bomb-laden Zero hit the *Kitkun Bay* (CV-71), causing considerable damage. Two others dived on the *Fanshaw Bay* (CV-70), but were shot down by antiaircraft fire, while others attacked the *White Plains* (CV-66). One of the kamikazes damaged by antiaircraft fire turned and crashed into the *St. Lo* (CVE-63). In little more than

Intrepid operating off the Philippines, 1944. Note the Hellcat fighter parked on an outrigger forward of her island.

UNITED STATES NAVAL INSTITUTE

30 minutes, the *St. Lo* sank, with the loss of about 100 men. It was a taste of the future for the fast carriers. As a young kamikaze pilot wrote on the eve of his sacrifice, "I am nothing but a particle of iron attracted by a magnet—the American aircraft carrier." The hectic pace of operations left Task Force 38 at the end of its endurance. The fast carriers were almost out of ammunition and food, which unlike fuel could not be replenished at sea. Even so, they stayed on for a few more days covering Leyte and attacking targets in the Philippines. Pilot fatigue was chronic. Although control of air operations passed to the Army, General Kenney could get only one group of P-38 Lightning fighters in operation from the rain-soaked airfields on Leyte. These fighters, used for combat air patrol over Leyte, did not provide close air support for the ground troops. Continuing Japanese air raids caused MacArthur to request that both the fast carriers and the escort carriers stay on for a while longer. Bogan's Task Group 38.2 and Davison's Task Group 38.4 were ordered to strike Visayan and Luzon targets, which were hit 28–30 October.

On 29 October, a Japanese kamikaze headed toward the *Intrepid*, straight at gun tub No. 10 on the port side, which was manned by an all black crew. The gunners continued to fire at the incoming aircraft, shooting away its left wing, but the damaged plane crashed into their position, killing ten men and badly burning others. Later, the official action report noted that "The crew of 20mm tub No. 10 remained at their guns, firing and servicing their guns until the plane struck them, even though towards the last it was apparent that the plane was going to strike their gun tub. Not one man deserted his gun or attempted to escape. It is very probable that the fire of this gun tub prevented the Japanese dive-bomber from crashing into the flight deck. Their heroic action reflects the highest spirit, courage and devotion to duty." Captain Bolger recommended the survivors of the attack for the Navy Cross, but they were awarded the Bronze Star instead due to the racial prejudice of the times. It was not until 1993, 49 years after the attack, that five of the surviving crew were finally awarded the Navy Cross.

Later that same day, a second casualty occurred while planes were landing. It was dark and raining, with a strong wind blowing. A Helldiver from the *Hancock* had approached too much to starboard and on touchdown the propeller apparently caught the edge of the catwalk, causing the plane to flip upside down near the forward after radio antenna mast. It began burning, but the flames were quickly put out by a repair party.

After successfully warding off a Japanese submarine attack, these task groups were hit hard by the kamikazes.

A Helldiver landing on *Intrepid* while operating off the Philippines, 1944.

(top) Gun Tub 10 in flames after being crashed by a kamikaze, 29 October 1944.

(bottom) Crew members cleaning up Gun Tub 10 after the flames have been extinguished, 29 October 1944.

On 30 October the *Franklin* and *Belleau Wood* were crashed. The *Franklin* had quickly eliminated two of the five planes attacking her, but the remaining three continued to bore in through the thick antiaircraft fire. One plane missed and splashed near the starboard side, another crashed into the *Franklin*'s flight deck, setting the deck afire. A fighter nearby fell through the damaged flight deck to the hangar deck below, starting more fires. The third aircraft slipped to within 30 feet of the *Franklin* before splattering into the aft end of the *Belleau Wood*'s flight deck. On *Franklin*, 56 died and 60 were wounded, but all fires were under control within two hours. The kamikaze that fell on *Belleau*

Wood started fires, setting off ammunition. Before the fires were brought under control, 92 men had died or were missing. Both carriers returned to Ulithi for temporary repairs before sailing for the West Coast. They would not be back in action until 1945.

That same day, Slew McCain relieved Pete Mitscher as commander of Task Force 38, with Rear Admiral Alfred E. Montgomery taking over as commander of Task Group 38.1. Davison's task group was released to head for Ulithi along with the escort carrier groups on 29–30 October. The Fifth Air Force was scheduled to fly in a group of medium bombers a week later, but rain had delayed airfield construction so much that they were postponed until December. At the end of the month only Bogan's three carriers and a handful of Army P-38s and P-61 night fighters were left to cover Leyte.

The slender air defenses over Leyte had invited a Japanese counterattack, which struck 1 November. The attack caused American commanders to send Sherman's Task Group 38.3 back to join Bogan's Task Group 38.2 in protecting shipping off Leyte, and Montgomery's Task Group 38.1 soon followed. The three task groups attacked Japanese airfields on Luzon on 5 and 6 November, taking the Japanese by surprise. The Japanese lost more than 400 planes, most of them on the ground. Halsey lost 25 carrier aircraft. The *Lexington* took a hit when a group of kamikazes that had avoided the Combat Air Patrols by hiding in cloud cover dived on the carriers. On 11 November, a strike of several hundred carrier planes attacked a convoy carrying 10,000 Japanese troops to Leyte, sinking five transports and four escorting destroyers. Task Force 38 stayed on, attacking Luzon

On the night of 30 November 1944, a Helldiver from the *Hancock* caught the edge of the catwalk on landing, causing the plane to flip upside down into the catwalk near the forward after radio antenna mast.

(above) Helldivers of VB-18 on patrol over the Philippine Sea, 15 November 1944. Note the crudely repainted markings on their tails.

(left) Rear Admiral Gerry Bogan, commander of Task Group 38.2 on the bridge of his flagship *Intrepid*, operating off the Philippines in November 1944.

airfields and shipping throughout November. On the 13th and 14th, the fast carriers sank a light cruiser and five destroyers plus seven merchant ships, destroying over 75 planes. Five days later they returned to shoot up more aircraft on the ground.

Sherman's Task Group 38.3 eventually returned to Ulithi, where it was joined by Davison's Task Group 38.4. A final strike on Luzon by Montgomery's Task Group 38.1 and Bogan's Task Group 38.2 marked the end of fast carrier operations in support of Leyte. The bombing aircraft destroyed several enemy planes and ships, including a heavy cruiser, but the kamikazes struck again on 25 November, hitting the *Intrepid*, *Essex*, and *Cabot*, and damaging the *Hancock* with a near-miss. Two Val dive bombers made suicide runs on the *Hancock* and *Cabot* but were splashed nearby. The *Essex* received her first major battle damage of the war when a lone kamikaze made it though the antiaircraft fire, skimmed the flight deck, and crashed into the port side. Fifteen men were killed and 44 wounded, but less than 30 minutes later, the fires had been put out and the flight deck was operational. The *Cabot* was also hit by two kamikazes and suffered minor fires and damage. The *Intrepid*, the "Hardluck I," did not get off as lightly and she earned another ticket to the West Coast—the hard way.

The destroyer *Wedderburn* (DD-684) refueling from *Intrepid*, 18 November 1944.

STRUCK OFF THE PHILIPPINES

AROUND NOON ON 25 NOVEMBER 1944, WITH THE APPROACH OF A bogie 19 miles out, the *Intrepid* went to general quarters at 1215. About that same time the combat air patrol from the *Hancock* intercepted and shot down a Zero and a Frances (a twin-engine bomber). As the *Intrepid* turned into the wind to launch a strike, her combat information center reported that three Vals were spotted by friendly fighters over the formation, one of which was shot down. Meanwhile, a returning strike

Intrepid going into an evasive turn as Japanese planes start a low-level attack, 25 November 1944.

was circling over the formation waiting for the *Intrepid* to complete the launching of her strike. At 1231 another attack was reported and a few minutes later a Zero exploded 2,000 feet above *Hancock*, the bomb from the plane landing on her port side forward. Another bomb was seen to land close aboard the *Cabot's* port side shortly afterward. No more enemy planes were reported until 1252 when the *Intrepid's* after fire control director picked up two Zeros astern at about 8,000 feet and gliding toward her. The two Zeros, now at about 100 feet, were jinking as they passed through the screen. The after 5-inch batteries opened up, followed by the 40-mm and 20-mm guns, bringing down one of the Zeros at 1,500 yards out.

While this was going on, there were friendly planes in the landing pattern and a hold fire order was given to avoid hitting them, but the starboard 40-mm and 20-mm batteries brought down yet another Zero. The Zero, approaching from the stern, managed to evade one of the Hellcats trying to cut him off, but the after

40-mm and 20-mm guns continued to fire despite the hold fire order. They started this Zero burning but could not bring him down in time. At 1,000 yards astern he went into a power stall and executed a wingover at 500 feet. The plane's bomb penetrated the flight deck and exploded in a vacant pilot ready room, killing 32 men in an adjacent compartment. The *Intrepid* executed a hard starboard turn to spill water and flaming gasoline over the side as fire fighting parties ducked exploding ammunition. The billowing smoke acted as a beacon and, a few minutes later, other enemy aircraft were spotted boring in from the port quarter. At this point, the ship's frustrated gunnery officer shouted, "For God's sake, are we the only ship on the ocean?" During the starboard turn the wind blew smoke across the flight deck, alternately blanking the guns on the starboard and then the port side. Although on fire, the Zero machine-gunned the deck, released its bomb, and struck the flight deck, sliding toward the bow and starting more fires. The firefighting parties battled the flames

Antiaircraft fire from *Intrepid* set this Japanese Zero afire. Still burning, it passed over the fantail before crashing, 25 November 1944

Flames, smoke, and debris rise from
Intrepid's flight deck after she was crashed
by a Japanese Zero, 25 November 1944.

Smoke rises from fires on *Intrepid* after being hit
by two kamikazes, 25 November 1944.

The crew of *Intrepid* putting out a fire on the flight deck caused by a kamikaze, 25 November 1944.

The damage on the hangar deck was extensive, with several aircraft destroyed.

UNITED STATES NAVAL INSTITUTE

and exploding ordnance for the next three hours and the aircraft of her air group were forced to land on other carriers or airfields at Leyte. The flight deck was ripped apart and the hangar deck was reduced to a twisted mass of hot steel plate. Sixty-five men died in the attack.

At the time of the attack, the *Intrepid* had 75 aircraft airborne, which were forced to land on the *Essex*, *Hancock*, and *Ticonderoga*. After refueling, they had flown ashore to Tacloban airfield on Leyte and participated in a strike before flying on to Ulithi, where the men of the air group expected to learn that the *Intrepid* had been sunk. The day after the attack, the *Intrepid* buried her dead at sea as she headed for Ulithi. Of the aircraft that were on board during the attack, only one, a Hellcat, was left in flyable condition. It was flown to the *Hancock* that same day.

The *Intrepid* arrived at Ulithi on 29 November and the following day Halsey visited to personally inspect the damage. The orphans of Air Group 18 also flew in that day and the pilots and air crew spent the night on board. As an old saying went, "Pilots like to sleep in their own beds." The next day the air group was detached and the *Intrepid*, escorted by two destroyers, headed for Pearl Harbor, where she arrived on 11 December. After five days assessing the damage, she headed for Hunters Point, arriving 20 December, just in time for Christmas. By this time, the Hunters Point shipyard personnel had begun to regard the *Intrepid* as "their" carrier and set about making her ready for battle again. Besides repairing all the damage, another quad 40mm mount was added to the stern in an enlarged sponson and new fire control equipment was added. Her repairs and modifications completed, the *Intrepid* put to sea on 11 February 1945 for her post-repair sea trials. With their successful completion, she pulled into Alameda two days later and got ready to embark a new air group.

On 15 February, Captain Giles E. Short relieved Captain Bolger. (Another early naval aviator, Short had served as air group commander on the *Enterprise* before the war and commanded the escort carrier *Bogue* in the Atlantic, serving as commodore of a task group. He would command the *Intrepid* for the rest of the war.) On

A burial party assembled on *Intrepid*'s hangar deck in the Philippine Sea the day following the 25 November 1944 kamikaze attack.

Avengers, Hellcats, and Helldivers of *Intrepid*'s Carrier Air Group 18 at Peleliu, 27 November 1944.

Intrepid undergoing repair at Hunters Point, December 1944.

the following day Air Group 10 under Commander John J. Hyland reported aboard. (Hyland was serving with a patrol squadron in the Philippines at the start of the war and later served as the personal pilot for Admiral King. He went on to command the Pacific Fleet after the war before retiring in 1971 as an admiral.) Air Group 10 differed from preceding air groups that had served on board the *Intrepid* in that it had an additional fighter-bomber squadron and the number of dive bombers and torpedo bombers was reduced. Both VF-10 and VBF-10 were equipped with the F4U Corsair. These changes in the composition of carrier air groups had been made to provide more fighters to counter the kamikaze threat. After its work up, the *Intrepid* again headed for Pearl Harbor, arriving on 2 March, where she embarked personnel from VF-86 bound for the *Wasp*. In company with the carriers *Franklin* and *Bataan*, the battle cruiser *Guam* (CB-2), and eight destroyers, she headed once again for Ulithi.

Arriving 13 March, the *Intrepid* was assigned to Rear Admiral Arthur W. "Raddy" Radford's Task Group 58.4. Operation Iceberg, the invasion of Okinawa, was scheduled for 1 April 1945. Okinawa was only 700 miles from Kyushu, the southernmost of the Japanese home islands, and would serve as the base for the eventual invasion of Japan. At Spruance's recommendation, the carrier task forces would replenish not only fuel at sea, but also ammunition and stores. Thus, the Fifth Fleet would become the "fleet that stayed" for the upcoming landings. Task Force 58's mission was to prepare for the landings by eliminating or reducing the threat from any remaining Japanese air or naval forces. The first target would be airfields and facilities on Kyushu.

JAPAN AND OKINAWA

TASK FORCE 58 LEFT ULITHI ON 14 MARCH, REPLENISHING AT SEA on the 16th. The next day, Japanese search aircraft located Task Force 58 while it was 160 to 175 miles from Kyushu, giving the Japanese time to disperse their aircraft to other locations. Task Force 58 struck airfields in the Kyushu area the next day. While steaming northwest toward southern Kyushu, the task force was scouted during the night by a number of Japanese aircraft. Early the next morning, the *Intrepid* launched a fighter sweep, then at 0700 launched the first strike against

Off Kyushu, a Japanese Betty got through heavy antiaircraft fire to crash close aboard the *Intrepid*, causing superficial damage, 18 March 1945.

The same Japanese Betty as photographed by *Enterprise*, 18 March 1945.

the airfield at Oita. Subsequent enemy air attacks by twin and single engine aircraft continued for two hours. At about 0806 a gleaming Betty bomber penetrated the screening formation, passed a cruiser at 3,000 yards, and headed for the *Intrepid* at about 500 feet when it started a shallow glide, apparently aiming at her starboard waterline. The five-inch and 40-mm guns on that side opened up, with the 20-mm guns holding their fire until about 1,500 yards. The kamikaze seemed as if it could not be stopped, but at the last moment before impact, a five-inch shell knocked its tail off, sending it end over end. It crashed into the sea while close aboard and fragments from the aircraft struck the forward bay on the starboard side, causing minor damage. The fire on the hangar deck was quickly brought under control, but gunfire from other ships in the task group attempting to bring down the enemy plane caused damage to

the *Intrepid*. A five-inch shell burst close aboard the port quarter, killing one man and wounding an officer and 43 men.

Throughout the day the *Intrepid* launched strikes and sweeps against the airfields at Usa, Tsuiki, Una Jima, and Oita. After bombing hangars and barracks with few Japanese aircraft getting caught on the ground, Mitscher sent his crews farther inland looking for targets. At Kobe and Kure they spotted several fleet units, including the super battleship *Yamato* and the aircraft carrier *Amagi*. That same day, the Japanese counterattacked; 50 Japanese aircraft hit Task Group 58.4 75 miles south of Shikoku. Early that morning, the *Enterprise* had a lucky escape when a bomb dropped on her failed to explode. Three Judy dive bombers attacked the *Yorktown* around 1300, hitting the signal bridge with a bomb that went through to the next deck

Japanese aircraft carriers under attack at Kure, 19 March 1945. The two larger carriers in center and at right are probably *Amagi* and *Katsuragi*. The smaller carrier between them is probably the escort carrier *Kaiyo*. The large ship at top left may be the incomplete carrier *Aso*. Note antiaircraft bursts in lower left.

The Western Pacific 1945

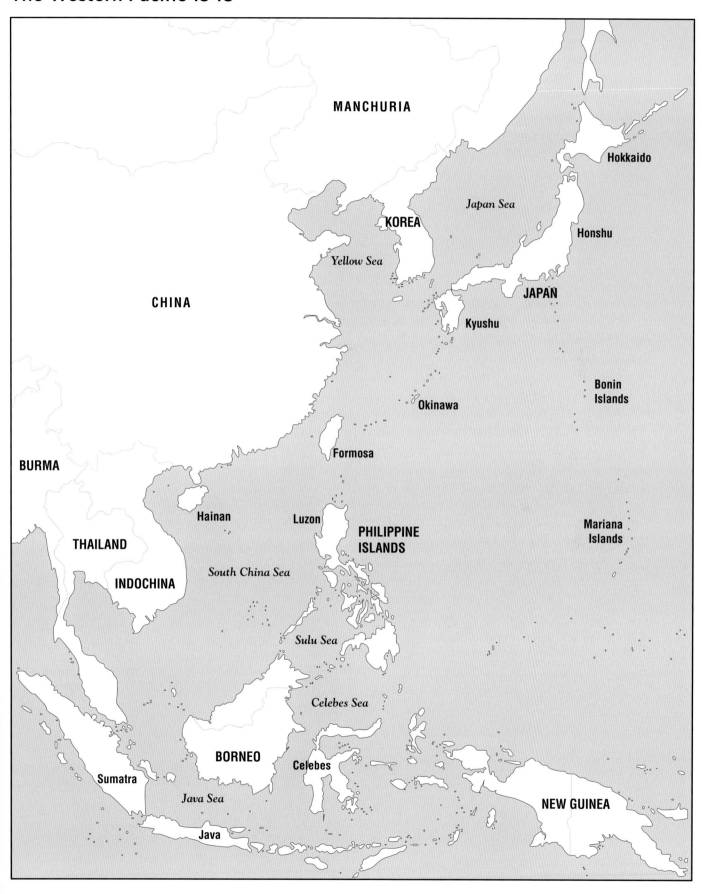

MANCHURIA

Hokkaido

Japan Sea

KOREA

Honshu

Yellow Sea

CHINA

JAPAN

Kyushu

Bonin
Islands

Okinawa

Formosa

BURMA

Hainan

Luzon

Mariana
Islands

THAILAND

PHILIPPINE
ISLANDS

INDOCHINA

South China Sea

Sulu Sea

Celebes Sea

BORNEO

Celebes

Sumatra

Java Sea

NEW GUINEA

Java

before exploding, leaving two gaping holes in her side. Five sailors died and 26 were wounded.

The next day, Task Force 58 again sent out strikes to the Inland Sea looking for shipping and naval units at Kobe and Kure. Antiaircraft fire was particularly intense around the naval installations and, although 17 ships including the *Yamato* and *Amagi* were hit, no serious damage was done. The Japanese counterattacked again in the early morning, hitting Task Group 58.2 hard. The *Wasp* was hit by an undetected aircraft and suffered heavy casualties: 101 killed and 269 wounded.

That same morning, the *Franklin* launched her second strike against Kure while a third was getting ready on the hangar deck below. A few minutes after seven, a lone Japanese aircraft appeared over the bow out of nowhere and dropped two 550-pound bombs on her flight deck. The first went through the flight deck near the forward elevator and exploded on the hangar deck; the second exploded on the flight deck amid aircraft warming up to launch. Both bombs started huge fires that were fed by the high-octane avgas in the plane's tanks. A series of explosions rocked the ship as bombs burst in their racks. Some of the aircraft in her air group carried the large 11.75-inch "Tiny Tim" rockets and, as the flames grew hotter, these began to go off. Hundreds were killed in the first blasts. By noon the fires were under control and her list stabilized. The heavy cruiser *Pittsburgh* (CA-72) moved in to take her in tow, but by early the next morning the *Franklin* had succeeded in regaining power and at noon the tow was cast off. The *Franklin* would be out of the war. With her departure the only other carrier armed with Tiny Tim rockets was the *Intrepid*. Results with the large inaccurate rockets were inconclusive and they were withdrawn from the carriers after the Okinawa operation.

After the 19 March attacks on the *Wasp* and *Franklin*, Task Force 58 slowly retired on a southerly course. Mitscher sent fighter sweeps over the Kyushu airfields to keep Japanese aircraft grounded, but in the afternoon of 21 March, Task Group 58.2, still protecting the crippled *Franklin*, again came under attack. This time flaming debris from a downed Zero kamikaze crashed into the destroyer *Halsey Powell* (DD-686) while she was alongside the *Hancock* refueling. Late that afternoon, 15 to 20 Japanese aircraft closed in on the *Enterprise*. Their bombs missed, but friendly antiaircraft fire caused a flight-deck fire, severely hampering her ability to conduct

night flying operations. Japanese aircraft continued to shadow the task force throughout the night and around 1400 the following day a large Japanese force was detected to the northwest. About 150 aircraft intercepted a group of 48 enemy aircraft 60 miles from the task force. Eighteen of the Japanese aircraft were twin-engine Betty bombers carrying the new Ohka one-man piloted bomb. Capable of speeds up to 600 miles an hour, the Ohka was almost impossible to shoot down once launched. The Americans later dubbed the Ohka bombs "baka" (fool, in Japanese). The payload made the Bettys difficult to maneuver, however, and easy prey for the defending fighters. No Japanese aircraft got through the fighter screen to the task force.

On 22 March Task Force 58 replenished and was reorganized into three task groups, leaving Task Group 58.2 as a "cripple" task group to escort the damaged *Franklin*, *Enterprise*, and *Wasp* back to Ulithi. Task Group 58.1 now included the *Hornet*, *Belleau Wood*, *San Jacinto*, and *Bennington*. Task Group 58.3 now had the *Essex*, *Bunker Hill*, *Hancock*, *Bataan*, and *Cabot*, while Task Group 58.4 had the *Yorktown*, *Intrepid*, *Langley*, and the newly arrived *Independence*. Task Force 58 pilots had claimed 528 aircraft destroyed on the ground and in the air. These losses delayed a major Japanese

A Corsair of VF-10 in flight, probably over Okinawa.

The logistics capability of the U.S. Navy greatly increased its staying power during the Okinawa campaign, with strikes alternating with refueling and replenishment evolutions.

response to the Okinawa landings until 6 April. In the morning of 23 March, the *Intrepid* launched her first strike against southern Okinawa. No enemy air opposition was met, but results were generally poor and the planned afternoon strikes were canceled because of deteriorating weather conditions. Strikes were launched again the next day, and later that night the task group headed for a replenishment area. Strikes were launched against the Okinawa and Anami island groups on the 26th and against the Nansei Shoto group the next day. After refueling on the 28th, strikes were launched early

the following morning based on reports of Japanese fleet units rounding the coast of Kyushu, but no enemy ships were found and alternate targets were selected. That afternoon the *Intrepid* launched a fighter sweep against the airfields at Kagoshima, Tojimbara, Kanoya, and Ibusuki. The task force then headed south again to hit the Ryukus.

The carrier task groups settled into a routine of fueling and striking in rotation in the week before the 1 April landings, maintaining constant alert to air attack. Visual aircraft detection was necessary as the Japanese

Although the U.S. Navy had developed underway refueling before the war, Okinawa marked the first time that provisioning ships at sea with ammunition and other stores was accomplished.

had discovered that U.S. radar could detect neither single aircraft coming in low, nor small groups at very high altitude. While the fighters protected the fleet, the bombers worked over Okinawa. In addition, Task Group 58.1 sank a convoy of eight ships north of Okinawa on 24 March. With the air strikes, Okinawa got seven days of shelling by the bombardment ships. Beginning 24 March, and for the next three months, the escort carriers also provided support. With the fast carriers *Saratoga*, *Franklin*, and *Wasp* taken out of the war, the arrival of four British carriers on 25 March was most welcome. Task Force 57 took on the responsibility of neutralizing the Sakishima Gunto, the islands southwest of Okinawa used as a staging base for Japanese aircraft shuttling between Kyushu and Formosa.

Aircraft from the escort carriers and the fast carriers also covered the operations in the Kerama Retto, islets close to the southwestern tip of Okinawa seized before the main landings. Army Air Force B-29s struck Kyushu on 27 and 31 March to further isolate Okinawa from Japanese aerial attack, and in the last seven days of March, Task Force 58 flew 3,095 sorties. But the Japanese still managed to launch 50 or so raids against the American ships off Okinawa from 26 to 31 March. The Japanese, however, lost around 1,100 aircraft. Radar picket destroyers had been placed around Okinawa on various bearings to detect incoming raids and these ships would suffer greatly under kamikaze attack in the coming days. Task Force 57, the British carrier force, was positioned to the southwest, between Okinawa and Formosa, while Task Force 58 was between Okinawa and Kyushu.

The landings on 1 April went well—too well. The Japanese decided not to oppose the landings on the beaches, choosing instead to prolong the struggle and take as many American lives as possible. The pre-landing air strikes had delayed a major Japanese counterstrike, although a limited number of small-scale

The Japanese super battleship *Yamato* maneuvering frantically under attack as a bomb explodes off her port side, 7 April 1945.

but determined air attacks, including kamikazes and suicide boat attacks, had been made against ships off Okinawa. The breather did not last long. The Japanese planned to launch the first of their massed "kikisui" (floating chrysanthemum) kamikaze attacks, which were intended to destroy the American fleet. For Task Force 58, tied to Okinawa to protect the invasion, the trial by kamikaze was only beginning. The first of the kikisui attacks was launched the afternoon of 6 April, with the outer radar picket destroyers being the first to suffer. Before the end of the day, almost 900 planes had attacked the American fleet—at least 355 were kamikazes. On board the carriers the bombers were stowed and all the fighters scrambled. By nightfall the Americans had lost three destroyers, two ammunition ships, and one LST. At least eight destroyers, a destroyer escort, and a minelayer suffered major damage. Task Force 58 claimed 249 incoming planes downed and, of the 182 that had arrived over the fleet, 108 were shot down. Attacks continued the next day, although with reduced intensity. The battleship *Maryland* (BB-46), the destroyer *Bennett* (DD-473), and the destroyer escort *Wesson* (DE-184) were all rammed by kamikazes. The *Hancock* was attacked by a single kamikaze, which cartwheeled across her deck and into aircraft spotted on her forward flight deck, the enemy's bomb exploding on the port catapult. She managed to recover her aircraft at 1630 but had lost 72 killed and over 80 injured. The losses were not all one sided, however. That same day, Task Force 58 destroyed the world's largest battleship.

At the same time that the kikisui attacks were launched, the Japanese sent the remains of their once proud surface fleet on a suicide mission of its own. The super battleship *Yamato*, the cruiser *Yahagi*, and seven destroyers were to proceed at top speed to Okinawa. The *Yamato* had only enough fuel for a one-way trip and it was hoped that she could beach herself and sink as many of the American ships with her 18.1-inch guns as possible before being destroyed. The force left Kure on 6 April but was spotted by the submarines *Threadfin* and *Hackleback* around 2000 that evening. Alerted by the submarine contact reports, Mitscher prepared to deal with this new threat.

Mitscher had ordered his available task groups to take up position northeast of Okinawa and launched search-strikes, arming the Helldivers with 1,000- and 250-pound bombs, the fighters with 500-pound bombs, and the Avengers with torpedoes. Task Force 58 search aircraft spotted the *Yamato* force at 0823 on 7 April. Seaplanes trailed the *Yamato* force and guided the carrier aircraft in on the Japanese. The first attack started just after noon as Task Group 58.1 and Task Group 58.3 launched 280 planes, including 98 torpedo bombers, at the Japanese ships. The *Yamato* was hit with four torpedoes and she developed a list. More followed from Task Group 58.4 and the Japanese faced air attacks throughout the remaining daylight hours. By 1300, the cruiser *Yahagi* was dead in the water, the destroyer *Hamakaze* sunk, and the *Yamato* had already received two bomb hits and a torpedo hit. Within the next hour, she received another five torpedo hits. Listing heavily, with her steering impaired and losing speed, the *Yamato* was helpless against the onslaught of carrier aircraft and at 1423 rolled over, exploded, and sank. The *Yahagi* took another 12 bomb hits and nine torpedoes before going down. Of the seven destroyers, only three made it back to port. The *Intrepid's* contribution included 27 bombs (13 1,000-pounders and 14 500-pounders) dropped by VB-10. It was reported that "while only five explosions could be seen separately counted during the attack, only a few splashes were seen. It is estimated that 20 of the 27 bombs dropped struck the ship. The first drop struck the port quarter, another just aft of the stack, and others amidships." Her torpedo squadron, VT-10, reported putting one torpedo into the *Yamato's* port side amidships. Ten torpedoes were put into a destroyer, which sank, and one into another destroyer. VBF-10 finished off the crippled destroyer with strafing and four 1,000-pound bombs. Task Force 58 lost only 10 planes and 12 men.

The kamikazes, coming mostly from Kyushu, continued their relentless assault. The *Enterprise* was hit on 11 April and forced back to Ulithi for repairs. Japanese aircraft continued to heckle the task force, heading in and then turning away until at 1928 one decided to make a real attack on the *Intrepid*, taking it under attack with radar-controlled gunfire. It was shot down 4,000 yards off the starboard quarter. At 2330 after many alerts, another Japanese plane attacked the formation, coming in on the *Intrepid's* starboard beam at 5,000 feet. At 2,000 yards out it turned away but the *Intrepid* kept up radar-controlled and continuous automatic weapons gunfire until it burst into flame and crashed at 14,000 yards.

While the *Intrepid* was off Okinawa, news arrived that the commander-in-chief, President Roosevelt, had died on 12 April 1945. On first hearing of his death,

Two kamikaze coming in for attack on *Intrepid*. One explodes in a sheet of flame on deck at the same time that its bomb explodes nearby. The other plane explodes as a near miss. As seen from *Yorktown*, 16 April 1945.

Intrepid receives her fourth direct hit by a kamikaze while operating off Okinawa, 16 April 1945.

Intrepid on fire after the attack by kamikaze. Other ships of the task group are in the background as SB2Cs from *Bennington* are seen flying overhead, 16 April 1945.

Another view after being hit by a kamikaze. Taken from the battlecruiser *Alaska* (CB-1).

Two crewmen run up the debris-strewn flight deck, just after she was hit by a kamikaze, 16 April 1945.

Crewmen battle fires on the flight deck, 16 April 1945.

many troops ashore thought it might be a Japanese propaganda trick, but they soon learned it was not. The *Intrepid* held a memorial service on board on 15 April but no one had much time to mourn since Japanese attacks continued unabated. On 16 April, the *Intrepid* launched a strike against Kokubu and at 1330 before it returned, the CIC reported a massive attack inbound. The attack included 165 kamikazes and a like number of conventional dive bombers and torpedo planes.

Five planes singled out the *Intrepid* as their target. The first, a Tony (a Japanese Army fighter), made a glide bombing run from dead ahead at 5,000 yards and was taken under fire by the forward 5-inch guns, which were soon joined by the 40mm and 20mm guns. At 1,500 yards it started to burn and crashed off the bow. The second plane passed aft from starboard to port and was taken under fire by several ships. The third approached from astern and made a run on a nearby battleship. It was brought down by fire from both ships. At 1335 the fourth and fifth approached from dead astern. The 5-inch guns were engaging other targets and the pair was taken under fire at 3,500 yards by the 40mm and then the 20mm guns. One caught fire and crashed close aboard the starboard side. The other, hit and trailing smoke, struck the flight deck near the after elevator in a near vertical attitude with such force that the imprint of its

Corsair

The Vought F4U Corsair combined the smallest airframe possible with the most powerful engine then available, the R-2800 Double Wasp, and resembled a "blue baseball bat with wings." Designed before the war, it was the first aircraft to exceed 400 miles per hour in level flight but its protracted development kept it from operating from aircraft carriers until late in the war. In order to take full advantage of the R-2800's power, a large propeller was needed and, to provide the necessary ground clearance for the propeller, an inverted gull wing kept the fuselage at a reasonable ground angle and the landing gear at a manageable length. The use of the gull wing also reduced aerodynamic drag where the wing met the fuselage at a right angle. In order to make room for a large fuselage fuel tank, the cockpit in the original design was moved aft, restricting the pilot's view over the long nose. This change, combined with landing gear problems, made the Corsair difficult to bring aboard a carrier. By the time these problems were corrected, the Corsair had become the primary Marine fighter operating from shore bases and the Navy was reluctant to switch from the Hellcat, which had better carrier landing characteristics. The Corsair later won a place aboard the *Essex*-class carriers when its superior speed was needed to counter the kamikaze threat. The Corsair eventually replaced the Hellcat as the Navy's primary fighter, and it continued in service into the Korean War as a fighter-bomber.

An F4U-1D Corsair of VF-10 in flight near Okinawa, April 1945.

wings was smashed into the deck. The bomb it carried exploded on the hangar deck, starting a gasoline fire, but the *Intrepid*'s experienced fire fighters had the fires out in 51 minutes. As the *Intrepid* battled the fires, however, two Zeroes were drawn by the smoke and attacked from the starboard quarter. The first dropped a bomb that missed by 75 yards on the starboard side while the other Zero dropped a bomb that landed close aboard to port. Both were brought down by gunfire. Repairs to the flight deck began immediately so that the *Intrepid* was able to recover her aircraft three hours later, but about 40

planes on the hangar deck were so badly damaged that they had to be jettisoned. Eight crewmen were killed, one was missing, and twenty-one were wounded. The *Intrepid* was ordered to the refueling area to assess her damage. The next morning it was determined that her operational capability had been greatly reduced and she was ordered to Ulithi for temporary repairs. Funeral services were conducted at sea on 18 April while she was en route to Ulithi. After her arrival on 20 April, previously undiscovered damage was found and she was ordered back to the West Coast via Pearl Harbor.

The hangar and gallery deck sustained considerable damage during the attack. About 40 planes were so badly damaged that they had to be jettisoned, as can be seen with this destroyed Corsair.

Intrepid suffered eight crewmen killed, one missing, and 21 wounded. Funeral services were held off elevator 2 on 18 April 1945.

WAR'S END

THE *INTREPID* DEPARTED ULITHI ON 4 MAY AND ARRIVED AT PEARL
Harbor on the 11th. After loading cargo and passengers, she departed
on the 14th and arrived at San Francisco on 19 May. Air Group 10
was detached at Alameda, and the *Intrepid* entered drydock at Hunters
Point. Hunters Point worked to get "their" carrier ready in time to "keep
her date in Tokyo." With Air Group 10 re-embarked, she left for Pearl
Harbor on 29 June 1945. After arriving on 5 July, the *Intrepid* spent the
rest of the month working up in preparation for the
final assault on Japan. On 30 July, accompanied
by two destroyers, she headed for Eniwetok, launching
strikes against the bypassed Wake Island on 6 August before arriving
at Eniwetok the next day. On 15 August, word was received of the
Japanese surrender, and she got underway on 21 August with the *Cabot*
and the new *Antietam* to support the occupation of Japan.

Intrepid, with cargo and passengers on
board, steamed through the Golden Gate
on her way to the Navy Yard, 19 May 1945.

UNITED STATES NAVAL INSTITUTE

After their rendezvous with Task Force 38 off the east coast of Japan, the *Intrepid* and *Cabot* were ordered to Okinawa where they became part of Task Force 72 on 30 August. Task Force 72 was to stand ready to respond to any hostile action on the part of isolated Japanese air or naval forces, but as it turned out no organized resistance occurred. On 1 September, the *Intrepid* left Okinawa with Task Force 72 and headed for the Yellow Sea. As she launched her planes for a show of force over Korea and northern China, the Japanese were signing the surrender documents on board the battleship *Missouri* in Tokyo Bay.

For the rest of September and into early October, the *Intrepid* operated in the Yellow Sea, supporting landings in Korea and China while Air Group 10 made show-of-strength flights over the Chinese cities of Shanghai, Chinwangtao, Tientsin, Tsingtao, and Peking. She departed on 8 October for Saipan for more shows-of-strength until 21 October when she headed for Japan. Finally, on 2 December 1945, the *Intrepid* left for the long journey home. At the end of World War II, the *Intrepid*'s gunners were credited with destroying 13 enemy aircraft and assisting in the destruction of five others. Her air groups shot down 160 enemy aircraft and destroyed 86 more on the ground, sank 11 ships, damaged 41, and probably sank two more. She earned the China Service, American Campaign,

Hunters Point Navy Yard workers were eager to get "their" carrier back in fighting shape, June 1945.

Asiatic-Pacific Campaign (with five battle stars), World War II Victory, Navy Occupation Service, and National Defense Service medals.

Air Group 10 detached on the *Intrepid*'s arrival at San Pedro on 15 December 1945 and the ship entered inactive status. On 4 February 1946 she shifted to

A Helldiver of VB-10 flies over Tientsin, China, as the city is reoccupied by the Allies, 5 September 1945.

Inchon Harbor, photographed from an *Intrepid* Helldiver as Allied forces begin the occupation of southern Korea, 8 September 1945.

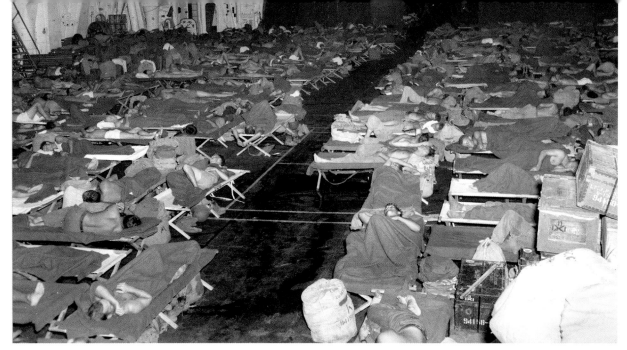

Personnel being transported back to the States on board *Intrepid* during Operation Magic Carpet, 1945.

San Francisco Bay. Captain Robert E. Blick, who had relieved Captain Short in January, remained in command until the *Intrepid* was designated a unit of the San Francisco Group of the Pacific Reserve Fleet "in commission in reserve" on 15 August 1946. The *Intrepid*'s first commanding officer during this period was Captain Henry G. Sanchez, who relieved Captain Blick on 11 April 1946 after having served five months as executive officer. He was relieved in November by Commander Arthur A. Giesser, who, along with eight other officers and a handful of enlisted men, prepared the *Intrepid* for complete deactivation by rust proofing and weather proofing her guns and machinery. On 22 March 1947 her status was changed to "out of commission in reserve" as a unit of the Pacific Reserve Fleet.

Space was at a premium during Magic Carpet operations. Personnel are seen here slinging hammocks in any available space.

Hunters Point

The Hunters Point Naval Shipyard was a U.S. Navy shipyard located on 638 acres of waterfront at Hunters Point in the southeast corner of San Francisco. Originally a commercial shipyard established in 1870, it was purchased and built up in the late 19th and early 20th century by the Union Iron Works company, later owned by the Bethlehem Shipbuilding Company, and named Hunters Point Drydocks, located at Potrero Point. The Navy purchased the shipyard in 1940, a year before the attack on Pearl Harbor, and began operations the next year as the San Francisco Naval Shipyard. It was operational until 1974 when it was deactivated and renamed Hunters Point Naval Shipyard. It was used commercially until 1986 when it was again taken over by the Navy as the home port of the *Missouri* battlegroup, under the name Treasure Island Naval Station Hunters Point Annex. The base was declared redundant as part of the Base Realignment and Closure (BRAC) effort in 1991 and was closed permanently in 1994.

An aerial view of the San Francisco Naval Shipyard at Hunters Point as seen from 7,000 feet, 24 May 1945. *Intrepid* is visible in the center, with the Crane Ship No. 1 (ex-USS *Kearsarge* [BB-5]) on her port side. The light aircraft carrier *Cabot* (CVL-28) is visible in the drydock in the lower half of the picture.

World War II Quote

From *USS* Intrepid *(CV 11) Cruise Book 1963—Twenty* INTREPID *Years 1943–1963*

The *Intrepid* earned many nicknames during the war. She was called the "Drydock I" because of the many times her damages had forced her to retire to one. She was called the "Evil I" because of her propensity to collect Japanese torpedoes, bombs, and Kamikazes, which she did more often than any other carrier that stayed afloat. But more than any nickname, her own name, the *Intrepid*, best described her behavior throughout the war. She was bombed, torpedoed, strafed, and crashed by Kamikazes; she was ripped open, burned, and twisted; she lost a great many men on her decks and in the air, but she always came back and fought again, boldly, undaunted, fearlessly and courageously, again and again and again. . . . Every time the Japanese sighted her it was as though a ghost had appeared. They had reported her as sunk several times, and yet it seemed she was always back to hurt them, and hurt them she did. For every wound she took she repaid the Japanese a hundredfold. She would not die and she could not be shaken off the Japanese throat that she had come to get. She would not quit. In the end it was the *Intrepid* that sat quietly in Tokyo Bay . . . after the Japanese had surrendered. *Intrepid* was one, there were many others, this happens to have been her chapter.

REBIRTH

HER DECOMMISSIONING IN 1947 WOULD NOT BE THE END OF THE *Intrepid*'s story. Five years later on 9 February 1952, she was again placed "in commission in reserve" under Captain Benjamin B. C. Lovett at San Francisco. The ceremony was highlighted by a speech given by Vice Admiral Sprague, her first skipper, who became Commander, Naval Air Force, Pacific Fleet in 1952. His remarks noted that she would be extensively modernized and again would be ready for combat using the latest types of aircraft. She got underway on 12 March headed for

Norfolk via the Panama Canal and arrived 17 days after her departure. She would again be temporarily decommissioned in the Norfolk Naval Shipyard on 9 April 1952 for two years of extensive modernization under the SCB-27C program to enable her to operate the latest generation of jet aircraft. The Navy, recognizing the primary role played by the aircraft carrier in offensive operations, changed the designation of aircraft carriers from CV to CVA for "attack aircraft carrier." While undergoing modernization, the *Intrepid* was reclassified as an attack carrier, CVA-11, on 1 October 1952, and was recommissioned in reserve on 18 June 1954. During the recommissioning ceremony at Portsmouth, Virginia, Mrs. John H. Hoover, who had originally christened the ship in 1943, accompanied

the ship's new commanding officer, Captain William T. Easton. The *Intrepid*'s crew prepared her for sea duty, and on 16 September she moved to her new home port at the Naval Operating Base in Norfolk.

On 1 November, the *Intrepid* was underway for local operations with a token number of aircraft from Air Task Group 201 to test her new steam catapults. The air task group (ATG) was a type of air group during the 1950s composed of squadrons from other air groups. (Since the number of Navy carrier air groups was set by Congress, the Navy created air task groups to meet the surge in operational tempo caused by the Korean War.) These squadrons and detachments could be changed as needed based on operational requirements. For this purpose, ATG-201 included VF-14 flying the

Intrepid at Hampton Roads, Virginia, 18 June 1954, following her SCB-27C modernization.

F3D-2 Skyknight two-seat jet night fighter along with detachments of the usual specialized "overhead" aircraft, in this case VC-12's Detachment (Det.) 33 with the AD-4W three-seat airborne early warning version of the Skyraider, VC-33's Det. 33 with the night attack and radar countermeasures four-seat AD-4N, photo F2H-2P Banshees of VC-62 Det. 33, and the HUP-2 helicopters of HU-2 Det. 33.

Fighter pilots are seen using the escalator to the flight deck, one of the features of her SCB-27C modernization.

This first underway experience since her re-commissioning would be a memorable one. During an underway refueling of the destroyer *Pierce*, the Atlantic was so rough that at one moment crewmen could see the keel of the *Pierce* as she pitched alongside and the next could look down her smokestack. The refueling was completed, however, and even the saltiest members of the crew admitted that they had never experienced anything like it. In the coming months, the crew of the *Intrepid* would learn to take the turbulent Atlantic in stride.

Beginning in January 1955, the *Intrepid* conducted shakedown operations out of Guantanamo Bay, Cuba, and the following month Air Group 4 reported aboard to begin working up for deployment. While at Mayport, Florida, Captain George L. Kohr assumed command of the *Intrepid*. She departed 28 May 1955 with Air Group 4 for her first deployment to the Mediterranean with the Sixth Fleet. The squadrons that made up CVG-4 reflected the aircraft of that era. VF-22 and VA-44 were equipped with the F2H Banshee, while their sister fighter squadron, VF-173, operated the FJ-3 Fury, the naval version of the F-86 Sabre. The attack squadron, VA-45, flew the propeller driven AD-6 Skyraider. Rounding out the air group were detachments of specialized overhead aircraft. Det. 33 of composite squadron VC-4 provided night intercept capability with a specialized version of the Banshee, the F2H-2N. VC-12's Det. 33 flew the AD-4W three-seat version of the Skyraider to provide airborne early warning. VC-33's Det. 33 provided night attack and radar countermeasures capability with the four-seat AD-5N. Reconnaissance duties were performed by the photo F2H-2P Banshees of VC-62 Det. 33. VC-7 Det. 33 flew the AJ-2 Savage, a twin piston-engine attack plane with a turbojet in the tail. The Savage was designed to deliver atomic weapons and the detachment was redesignated as a heavy attack squadron, VAH-7, before the end of the deployment. The tandem-rotor HUP-2 Retriever helicopters of HU-2 Det. 33 performed various utility and rescue duties, such as acting as plane guards. This deployment would be one of the *Intrepid*'s longest. She traveled from one end of the Mediterranean to the other, with port visits to Cadiz and Valencia in Spain; Gibraltar; Livorno, Naples, and Rapallo in Italy; Athens, Salonika, and Rhodes in Greece; Marseille and Cannes in France; and Istanbul in Turkey before returning to Norfolk in November. During the stopover in Athens, Captain Paul P. Blackburn Jr. assumed command of the *Intrepid* on 15 August.

The first months of 1956 were taken up with routine operations in the Virginia Capes and off Mayport, Florida. Air Group 8 replaced Air Group 4 in March. The makeup of CVG-8 differed from that of CVG-4. Although the detachments of overhead aircraft were the same, the other squadrons flew different aircraft. VF-82 flew the F2H-4 version of the Banshee, while VF-61 flew the F9F-8 Cougar. (Captain Blackburn was the brother

Intrepid working up with Air Group 4 off Guantanamo Bay, Cuba, February 1955, before her first deployment to the Mediterranean.

An AD-5 Skyraider folds its wings and taxis forward after landing, April 1956. The AD-5 was a two-seat version of the Skyraider originally intended to be an antisubmarine hunter-killer, but was adapted to other roles.

(below) Gibraltar as seen from the hangar deck of the *Intrepid* during her second deployment to the Mediterranean, March 1956.

of John T. "Tommy" Blackburn, who gained fame during World War II leading VF-17, the Jolly Rogers, in the Solomons. VF-61 was the descendent of this famous Corsair squadron.) Attack squadron VA-83 flew the F7U-3M Cutlass, which was the first Navy aircraft to carry the Sparrow air-to-air missile, while VA-85 flew the AD-5 two-seat and AD-6 single-seat versions of the Skyraider. Her second deployment to the Mediterranean was from May to September 1956. Captain Forsyth Massey relieved Captain Blackburn in August. The *Intrepid* would enter a new phase of her career as she was about to undergo another major modernization.

SCB-27

The Ship Characteristics Board (SCB) was established in 1945 in the office of the Chief of Naval Operations to exert more operational influence on ship design decisions, and various modernization efforts were assigned SCB program numbers. Many of these applied to aircraft carriers. Originally, SCB-27 applied only to the completion of *Oriskany*, an *Essex*-class carrier left unfinished after the war, to an extensively revised design. The SCB-27 modernization required two years for each carrier and allowed operation of the much heavier, faster aircraft of the early jet era. The flight deck structure was reinforced, and stronger and larger elevators, much more powerful hydraulic catapults, and new Mark 5 arresting gear were installed. The original four twin 5-inch gun mounts were removed, clearing the flight deck of guns. The new five-inch battery included eight weapons, two on each quarter beside the flight deck, and twin 3-inch gun mounts replaced the 40-mm guns. The island was completely redesigned, and was taller, but shorter with the boiler uptakes angled aft. A single radar and communications pole mast was atop the island. The ready rooms, which had proved to be vulnerable during the war, were moved from the gallery deck to below the armored hangar deck. To move flight crews up to the flight deck, a large escalator was installed on the starboard side below the island. Other aviation features included increased aviation fuel capacity and faster pumping capability. Fire fighting capabilities were enhanced and electrical power generation, weapons stowage, and handling facilities were all improved. The armor belt

Intrepid **undergoing her SCB-27 C conversion.**

was removed and blisters were fitted to the hull sides to compensate, widening the beam by 8 to 10 feet and increasing displacement. The maximum speed was slightly reduced, to 31 knots. There were two versions of the SCB-27 program. The first, SCB-27A, featured a pair of H-8 hydraulic catapults, but by the time of the *Intrepid*'s modernization, the C-11 steam catapult had been adapted from the British BXS-1. The first ships equipped with the new steam catapults, the *Hancock* and *Ticonderoga*, used British-built versions. The *Intrepid* would be the first to use American-built steam catapults. The SBC-27C carriers were also equipped with jet blast deflectors, deck cooling, fuel blending facilities, an emergency recovery barrier, and storage and handling for nuclear weapons—which was not included in all of the SCB-27A carriers. The SCB-27C conversion also moved the aft elevator to the starboard deck edge, as was done with the *Intrepid* during her first modernization period at Newport News Shipbuilding from April 1952 to June 1954.

3-inch Guns

Toward the end of World War II, the Navy sought a more effective antiaircraft weapon. The 3"/50 was developed in 1944 when it was realized that the 20-mm and 40-mm guns were ineffective in stopping kamikazes. Since a 3-inch projectile was the smallest that could be fitted with a proximity fuze and the concentric recoil spring of the existing 3"/50 weapon lent itself to development of an automatic weapon, a crash program was initiated. The maximum range was under 15,000 yards with an antiaircraft ceiling of over 14,000 feet, and a rate of fire from 45 to 50 rounds per minute. With the end of the war development slowed, but by 1948 the 3"/50 was in widespread use throughout the Navy. A twin 3"/50 could fit in the same working circle as a 40-mm quad mount, but since it was heavier the new mount usually replaced 40-mm quad mount on a one-for-three basis. The 3"/50 was included in the SCB-27

A 3"/50 Mark 33 twin mount on the *Intrepid* in 1958 after her SCB-27C conversion.

program, but as time went on the number of mounts was reduced, as were the 5"/38 weapons to save weight.

Radar Postwar

The *Intrepid* received an entirely new radar suite during her 1952–1954 SCB-27C conversion. Air-search sets included the SPS-8 and the new SPS-12 with a 17-foot-by- 12-foot parabolic dish. It could detect aircraft at 90 nautical miles and over 40,000 feet. The SC-5, an improved SC series with anti-jamming features, was installed. The new SPN-6 CCA (carrier controlled approach) radar was also introduced. It was used for air traffic control and marshalling into the holding area. When the *Intrepid* was modernized under the Fleet Rehabilitation and Modernization (FRAM) program in 1966, she received the SPS-29 radar. It had a 7-foot by 4-foot "bedspring" antenna and a range of 270 nautical miles, about three times that of the SPS-12 it replaced. Air traffic control was also improved by the addition of the SPN-12 and SPN-55 sets. The *Intrepid* received a new height-finding radar, the SPS-30, during her FRAM overhaul. The 12-foot disc antenna of this "pencil beam" radar had a range of 240 nautical miles, or three times the range of the SPS-8, which it replaced. Ship detection was furnished by two SG surface-search sets that could detect large ships at over 20 nautical miles and aircraft under 500 feet at about

June 1956, atop the platform at the front of her stack is the SPS-8. The SPN-6 carrier controlled approach radar is on the port side of the yardarm halfway up the pole mast, with the SPS-12 to starboard and the SG above it. The parabolic radar antennas of the SPG-25 fire control radars have replaced the World War II–era Mark 4 and Mark 22 radars on the Mark 37 directors. The dome at the top of the pole mast is a TACAN (tactical aid to navigation) antenna.

UNITED STATES NAVAL INSTITUTE

15 nautical miles. Also, its displays of ships, as well as land masses, made it useful to navigation. Surface-search radar was also improved during the SCB-27C conversion. The SG-6 combined surface and zenith search in the same radar set. The antenna used two reflectors, a 7-foot-by-2-foot cut parabolic and a 5-foot solid dish. The surface-search capabilities of the parabolic antenna were comparable to the SG and the smaller dish was meant to scan the conical void space directly over the ship. The main radar improvement during SCB-125 was the addition of the SPS-10 replacing the last of the SG series sets. It had an 11-foot-by-3-foot parabolic reflector that could effectively range on the horizon and detect a periscope at up to 16,000 yards.

An F3D-2 from the VF-14 Top Hatters, 1954.

Skyknight

The Douglas F3D Skyknight was a twin-engine, mid-wing jet fighter designed as a carrier-based all-weather night fighter for the Navy and Marines. Although never produced in great numbers, it did see useful service as a land-based night fighter in Korea. Because its low-slung intakes tended to make it vulnerable to foreign object damage, it saw limited service on board carriers. Its association with the *Intrepid* was from September to November 1954 with VF-14 as part of ATG-201. The Navy's primary aim during this limited deployment was to test her new steam catapults.

Skyraider

The separate dive bomber and torpedo aircraft of World War II were replaced by a single attack aircraft, the Douglas AD Skyraider. The Skyraider was a single-seat piston-engine aircraft that had the performance of a World War II fighter and the ability to carry an amazing amount of ordnance. The "Able Dog" was powered by a 2,700-horsepower Wright R-3350 radial engine and armed with four 20-mm cannon in the wings. The Skyraider, described as a "dump truck with wings," performed a variety of roles. These special mission aircraft were identified by a suffix to the basic designation: N for all-weather, W for radar surveillance, or Q for electronic countermeasures. It served during the Vietnam war as the A-1 and was affectionately known as the "Spad."

A Skyraider of VA-45 makes a pass over the *Intrepid*, February 1955. Note the numerous underwing hardpoints for carrying ordnance.

Banshee

The McDonnell F2H Banshee, originally planned as a day fighter, featured twin Westinghouse J34 engines buried in the wing roots. The first production model, the F2H-1, entered squadron service in 1949. The F2H-2 model, with improved 3,200-pound thrust J34 engines, was used in combat over Korea. Known affectionately as the "Banjo," the F2H became the Navy's primary jet fighter-bomber and was adapted for a variety of missions, including photo reconnaissance and night fighter versions.

A Banshee on board *Intrepid* in January 1955. In the 1950s, the Navy briefly considered bare metal finishes for their carrier aircraft, but the corrosive effects of sea air soon led to the abandonment of the idea.

Retriever

The Piasecki HUP-2 Retriever, a compact, twin-tandem-rotor utility helicopter powered by a 550-hp Continental R-975-46 piston engine, was the standard shipboard helicopter for plane guard and utility work on carriers at the time the *Intrepid* was recommissioned. It was the first helicopter to have an autopilot to allow hands off hovering. Introduced in the early 1950s, the HUP-2 and HUP-3 versions served on board the *Intrepid* until her conversion to an ASW carrier in 1962.

A HUP-2 Retriever of helicopter utility squadron HU-2 Detachment 33 performs plane guard duty, May 1956.

An AJ Savage landing on *Intrepid*, February 1955.

Savage

In the immediate postwar era, the Navy developed the North American AJ-1 Savage to provide a nuclear attack capability. The Savage was powered by two 2,300-horsepower R-2800 piston engines with a 4,600-pound thrust Allison J34 jet engine in the tail to provide additional speed during an attack. These large aircraft would prove unpopular on carriers because of their impact on the rest of the air group and would eventually be modified for other roles, such as tanking and photo reconnaissance. They would be replaced in the heavy attack role by the jet-powered Skywarrior.

An F9F-8 of the VF-61 Jolly Rogers on the *Intrepid*'s port catapult, April 1956.

Cougar

The Grumman F9F-8 Cougar, powered by a single 7,250-pound thrust Pratt & Whitney J48 engine, was the swept-wing version of the Panther that had served in the Korean War. It was used primarily as a day fighter, but there were light attack and photo reconnaissance versions as well. Although the Cougar was replaced as a fighter on the carriers by the F11F Tiger and F8U Crusader in the late 1950s, training versions remained in naval service until 1974.

An F7U-3M Cutlass on the starboard catapult, May 1956.

Cutlass

The Vought F7U Cutlass was one of the most unorthodox aircraft ever to operate from a carrier. It was a tail-less, single-seat, twin engine jet with twin vertical tail fins but no horizontal tail surfaces. The first versions of the Cutlass were underpowered (leading to the nickname "Gutless Cutlass") and the introduction of improved engines was delayed. Although the F7U-3 version, powered by two 4,600-pound thrust Westinghouse J34 engines, could reach speeds exceeding Mach 1, the speed of sound, the radical design encountered previously unknown aerodynamic problems which earned it the nickname of "The Ensign killer." Few squadrons made deployments with the Cutlass, and most beached them ashore for part of the time during a cruise because of operational problems. The F7U-3M missile-armed variant that served on board the *Intrepid* was one of the first fighters to use the Sparrow air-to-air missile on carriers.

A GOLDEN AGE

ON COMPLETION OF HER SECOND DEPLOYMENT, THE *INTREPID* proceeded on 29 September 1956 to the New York Naval Shipyard where she was in drydock in Brooklyn for a major part of her yard period as she received her SCB-125 modifications. Captain Massey retained command while she was in the yard except for a brief period of temporary duty from October to November. By the end of April 1957, the *Intrepid* had a new angled flight deck and mirror landing system and was moved to Bayonne, New Jersey, for her final finishing

Intrepid alongside *Shasta* (AE-6) to replenish ammunition while operating in the North Atlantic near the Arctic Circle as part of NATO fall maneuvers, 22 September 1957.

touches in the last weeks of April. During this yard period her crew enjoyed liberty in New York and began their long association with the "Big Apple," adopting the nickname "Lucky 'Leven." A New York dancer and choreographer known for her work in television, Broadway theater, and movies, Thelma "Tad" Tadlock, was even named "Miss Intrepid of 1957."

The *Intrepid* got underway for Norfolk on 7 May. She then departed on the 20th for refresher training at Guantanamo. Air Group 6 joined her. Besides the usual fighter and attack squadrons—VF-71 with the F2H-3/4 Banshee, VF-33 with the FJ-3/3M Fury, VA-66 with the F9F-8B Cougar, and VA-25 with the AD-6 Skyraider—the various detachments that were previously part of composite squadrons were now redesignated to reflect their roles. The heavy attack detachment, VAH-11 Det. 33, was equipped with the AJ-1 Savage, which was capable of delivering atomic weapons, while VA(AW)-33 Det. 33 provided an all-weather attack capability with the AD-5N version of the Skyraider. VAW-12 Det. 33 performed airborne early warning with the AD-5W, and VFP-62 Det. 33 performed reconnaissance with the F9F-8P photo version of the Cougar. HU-2 Det. 33 again provided rescue and utility services with the HUP-2 Retriever helicopter.

For the next few months, the *Intrepid* operated in the Western Atlantic. During September, the *Intrepid* headed for her first visit to northern Europe and participation in the North Atlantic Treaty Organization's Operation Strikeback. The largest peacetime naval exercise up to that time, the ten-day exercise involved the navies of six countries and was designed to assess the capabilities of a carrier strike force operating in the North Atlantic to strike the northern flank of the Soviet Union in the event of an all-out Soviet attack on NATO. On 20 September, the *Intrepid* experienced another first when she crossed the Arctic Circle, thereby qualifying the ship's company and air group to become members of the Royal Order of the Blue Nose. On 4 October, while visiting Brest, France, Captain Joseph H. Kuhl assumed command from Captain Massey. The remainder of the year was spent in routine operations with short cruises to the Virginia Capes.

In December 1957, operating out of Norfolk with Air Task Group 181 on board, the *Intrepid* conducted Operation Crosswind, to study the effects of wind on carrier launches. At this time ATG-181 included VF-41 with F3H-2 Demon fighters, VF-81 and VA-76 flying the F9F-8/8B Cougar, VF-84 with the FJ-3/3M Fury, as well as detachments from VAW-12 Det. 33 with AD-5Ws, VA(AW)-33 Det. 33 with AD-5Ns, VFP-6 Det. 33 with F9F-8Ps, HU-2 Det. 33 with HUP-2s. As a result of these experiments, the *Intrepid* proved that under certain conditions carriers could safely conduct flight operations without turning into the wind and even launch planes while steaming downwind.

The following January, the *Intrepid* entered the Norfolk Naval Shipyard for needed repairs and upkeep and by May she was at sea operating in the local area with ATG-181, in preparation for operations with the Second Fleet in the North Atlantic. From 9 June to 8 August 1958, Naval Reserve midshipmen from various colleges and universities were on board. During this summer cruise the *Intrepid* also participated in Atlantic Fleet exercise (Lantflex) 1-58 and made

An F8U-1 Crusader making a touch-and-go on *Intrepid* during Operation Cross Wind, 11 December 1957.

port calls in Lisbon, Oslo, and Rotterdam. The *Intrepid* sailors also had the opportunity to visit the 1958 Brussels World's Fair. During the first and last week of the cruise, exercises against the East Coast tested the attack squadrons' ability to deliver their weapons on target and the ability of the fleet to defend against air attack; the exercises also tested the air defense systems ashore.

On 4 October 1958, Captain Paul Masterton assumed command. The *Intrepid* continued her Caribbean operations, visiting Barbados for four days during Lantflex 2-58. When Air Group 6 embarked for a month of local operations in November, it had different squadrons, some of which were flying new aircraft. Although the overhead detachments were the same, the fighter squadrons were now VF-41 with the F3H-3/3M Demon and VF-33, which had been re-equipped with the new F11F-1 Tiger. The attack squadrons were VA-42 with the AD-6 and VA-106 with the new A4D-2 Skyhawk. Her Caribbean operations completed, the *Intrepid* returned to Norfolk in November in time for the holidays.

She departed on 13 February 1959, and after a brief port call at Gibraltar, entered the Mediterranean on 3 March for six months of operations from one end of the Mediterranean to the other, with stops at various ports in Spain, Italy, France, and Greece. During this deployment there were more changes to CVG-6. The Demons of VF-41 were replaced by the F4D-1 Skyrays of VF-74. There were now two A4D-2 Skyhawk squadrons, VA-46 and VA-66, while the AD-6 squadron was now VA-25. The overhead detachments were the same and the F9F-8B squadron, VF-81, was gone. Turning over to the *Essex* at Pollensa Bay on the northern end of Majorca, one of Spain's Balearic Islands, the *Intrepid* again stopped briefly at Gibraltar before heading for Norfolk on 21 August. On her return on 30 August 1959 Captain Edward C. "Eddie" Outlaw assumed command of the *Intrepid* from Captain Masterson (During World War II, as skipper of VF-32 on the light carrier *Langley*, Outlaw became an ace in a day during a fighter sweep against Truk. Later he became air group commander and would eventually retire as a rear admiral.)

On 8 October 1959, the *Intrepid* began a four-month overhaul at the Norfolk Naval Shipyard for major repairs, including renovating the engineering plant, repairing the flight deck, replacing worn sea valves, propellers, rudder, and shafts. Major alterations included strengthening the hull structure and hangar deck, modernizing the antennas, and repainting the interior of the ship. She left the shipyard on 3 December to spend the holidays at the pier in Norfolk. In January, the *Intrepid* was ready for her post-yard shakedown in Guantanamo Bay, followed by a visit to the Dominican Republic. Returning to Norfolk, the newly commissioned super carrier *Independence* (CV-62) was moored across Pier 12 from the *Intrepid*. It seemed awkward to continue using her old title of "Mighty I," so she adopted a newer and better one, the "Fighting I."

The *Intrepid* and *Independence* (CVA-62) moored at Naval Operating Base (NOB) Norfolk, Virginia, while making last minute preparations for deployment to the Mediterranean.

AD-6 Skyraiders of VA-65 are in position on the bow catapults while an F11F-1 Tiger of VF-33 awaits the signal to taxi onto the catapult, 18 November 1960.

Meanwhile, the changes in CVG-6 from the year before would remain during local operations from February to March and operations in the Caribbean later that year from June to July.

On 4 August 1960, the *Intrepid* departed Norfolk for another Mediterranean cruise. In the words of Captain Outlaw, the *Intrepid* would have "two primary missions: combat readiness and building good will." She again deployed with CVG-6, but this cruise did not include the detachments of WF-2 Tracers from VAW-12 or the electronic warfare AD-5Q Skyraiders of VAW-33. She visited various ports in Italy, Turkey, Lebanon, and France, and on 8 September, while in port near Rome, Captain Charles S. "Charlie" Minter Jr. assumed command. On 17 February 1961, the *Intrepid* returned to Norfolk and February, March, and April were spent in the shipyard at Portsmouth. While there, a boiler explosion on board on 25 April injured 11. After completing carrier qualifications and loading ordnance, the *Intrepid* was ordered to New York, where she put on a demonstration of naval air power for a group of aviation space writers on 5 May, followed by guests from the Armed Forces Staff College, the Naval War College, the Army War College, the Inter-American Defense Board, and other guests of the Chief of Naval Information from 8 to 12 May.

On 24 May 1961 Captain James L. "Doc" Abbott Jr. relieved Captain Minter and on 1 June the ship was

A bow shot of *Intrepid* underway in the Mediterranean, 28 August 1961.

underway for the Caribbean to show support for U.S. South American policy following the assassination of Generalissimo Trujillo of the Dominican Republic. After a brief stop at Norfolk, the *Intrepid* arrived at New York on 1 July where she would be open to the public as well as act as host ship for the commander of the Second Fleet.

The *Intrepid* would again operate in the Atlantic with CVG-6, and with more changes to the air group. VF-162 was now the Skyray squadron and there were other changes as new aircraft became operational. VF-33 had traded its Tigers for the new Vought F8U Crusader. Another new squadron was VAH-13 flying the A3D Skywarrior, marking its debut on board the *Intrepid*, although it would not deploy with the air group on the next cruise to the Mediterranean.

The *Intrepid* departed on her final cruise to the Mediterranean as an attack carrier on 3 August 1961. Off the Azores on 8 August one of her helicopters developed mechanical trouble and crashed, although her crew was rescued. On the 16th she relieved the *Franklin D. Roosevelt* (CV-42) in the Gulf of Palmas off the southern tip of Sardinia. During the cruise she visited various ports in Italy, Greece, France, and Spain and participated in NATO exercises Checkmate I and II, Greenstone, and Big Game. On her way to Pollensa Bay, where she was to be relieved by the *Shangri-La*, a major storm delayed her arrival until 19 February. The next day she passed though the Straits of Gibraltar before continuing into the Atlantic, arriving at Norfolk on 1 March.

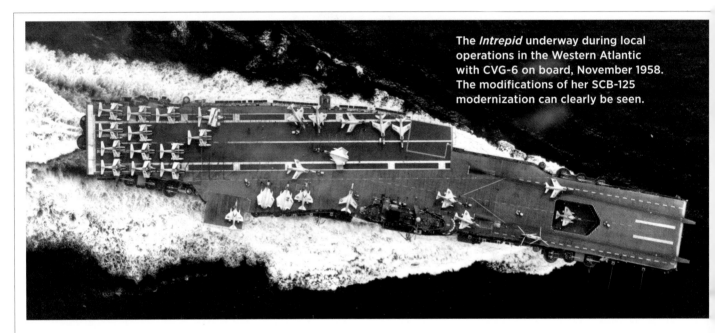

The *Intrepid* underway during local operations in the Western Atlantic with CVG-6 on board, November 1958. The modifications of her SCB-125 modernization can clearly be seen.

SCB-125

In addition to the steam catapult, another significant British innovation was the angled deck, a simple, but revolutionary concept that allowed aircraft "go arounds" without hitting the barricade. The Navy began to give the angled deck concept serious consideration in 1951 and in the spring of 1952, two carriers, the large carrier *Midway* and the *Wasp*, were given superficial modifications to test the concept. Later, the *Antietam* (CV-36), an essentially unmodified *Essex*-class carrier, became the Navy's first true angled-deck carrier. The SCB-125 program, which was intended to apply the angled deck to the *Essex*-class carriers, also included the fitting of an enclosed "hurricane" bow. The *Intrepid* got her SCB-125 modification between September 1956 and May 1957 at the New York Naval Shipyard in Brooklyn. The *Intrepid,* along with the *Ticonderoga* and *Hancock*, had some features that distinguished them from their sisters that had their SCB-27C and SCB-125 upgrades done at the same time: the starboard deck edge elevator was further aft and the hurricane bow had a noticeable "knuckle" compared to the smoother transition of the later modifications. After her SCB-125 conversion, the *Intrepid* also had an enlarged five-sided forward elevator.

To take advantage of the capabilities offered by the angled deck and the steam catapult, a new method of controlling aircraft as they came aboard had to be devised, since a landing signal officer could only control one aircraft at a time and the limitations of the human eye made control using paddles limited to no more than one-half mile. Fortunately, the British came up with a simple and elegant solution, the mirror landing system. It used a large mirror, concave around its horizontal axis, placed alongside the landing area at the edge of the angled deck. The mirror pointed astern at the angle of the glide path and was mounted on gimbals connected to the ship's fire-control system, which was gyro stabilized. This allowed the mirror to compensate for any movement of the ship. Aft of the mirror, a powerful light source was aimed at the mirror so that a cone of light was reflected back along the glide slope. The pilot would see a spot of light, the "ball," when he flew in the middle of the beam. To position his aircraft more precisely, a horizontal row of green datum lights was mounted on either side of the mirror. If the pilot was a little high on the glide path, the ball appeared to be slightly above the reference lights, if too low, the ball was below the reference lights. Later, the mirror was replaced by a Fresnel lens and colors added to the ball, but the principle was the same. Together, the three elements—angled deck, steam catapult, and mirror landing system—allowed the aircraft carrier to truly enter the jet age.

An F3H-3 Demon of the VF-41 Black Aces in 1961 while part of CVG-7 on board the *Independence*. VF-41 was part of CVG-6 on the *Intrepid* in 1958.

Demon

The McDonnell F3H Demon was a swept-wing, single-engine, single-seat fighter that was developed in parallel with the Skyray. The Demon first flew in 1951 and early models were underpowered and accident prone. After production of the improved F3H-2 began in 1955, the fighter found its place in carrier air wings. The F3H-2M missile-armed version was equipped with Sparrow air-to-air missiles. Four Sparrows could be carried, but a full load was rarely carried by fleet aircraft because their weight seriously affected performance. Although not supersonic, the Demon complemented day fighters such as the Vought F8U Crusader and Grumman F11F Tiger as an all-weather, missile-armed interceptor.

An F11F of the VF-33 Astronauts lands on the *Intrepid* during Operation Big Deal in the Mediterranean, February 1959.

Tiger

The Grumman F11F-1 was developed to incorporate new aerodynamic concepts, such as area rule, and other advances to the Cougar design. In the end, the Tiger was a completely new aircraft. Although supersonic, the Tiger's carrier service lasted only four years because of its engine reliability problems and lack of range and endurance. Tigers served in seven Navy fighter squadrons and its place was taken by the superior Crusader, which entered fleet service at about the same time in 1957.

The Skyhawk had a long and illustrious career. This view shows a Scooter about to launch from the *Intrepid* while in the Gulf of Tonkin, September 1968.

Skyhawk

The Douglas A4D Skyhawk and the A3D Skywarrior were the Navy's first jet attack aircraft, with the A4D Skyhawk at the opposite end of the scale. Powered by a single 11,200-pound thrust Pratt & Whitney J52 engine, it was remarkable for its small size. Its short span delta wings did not need folding and with its tall tricycle landing gear it could carry a wide variety of ordnance, including the new,

smaller nuclear weapons. It was known as the "scooter" and through various versions remained in production until 1979 and served with many air forces around the world. Skyhawks served on the *Intrepid* during her service as an attack carrier and again as the A-4 during her deployments off Vietnam. Later in her career, detachments were on board during deployments in the Atlantic and Mediterranean to act as her "fighter" protection.

Plane handlers position an F4D-1 Skyray of VF-74 onto the port catapult on the *Intrepid* during a Mediterranean cruise in May 1959.

Skyray

As the Navy's first delta wing fighter, the Douglas F4D Skyray was a single-seat, single-engine high-performance interceptor that sacrificed endurance for rate of climb and speed to counter the threat of high-altitude bomber attacks on carriers. After the engine of the original design was changed to a more powerful 9,700-pound thrust Pratt & Whitney J57 and other modifications the "Ford," as it soon became known, began capturing flight records. In addition to serving in Navy and Marine all-weather fighter squadrons, the F4D also served with a shore-based Navy all weather fighter squadron as part of the North American Air Defense Command, a predominantly Air Force organization.

Crusader

The Vought F8U Crusader with its 10,700-pound thrust Pratt & Whitney J57 with afterburner was truly a supersonic fighter that had several innovative design features,

such as a variable incidence wing, which increased the angle of attack for greater lift during carrier launches. The Crusader was the last Navy fighter designed with cannons

as its primary armament, although it had launch rails on "cheek" pylons for Sidewinder air-to-air missiles. It was not an easy aircraft to fly and although it took a catapult shot well,

The Crusader's service on the *Intrepid* included Vietnam. Seen here is an F-8C of VF-111 Detachment 11 ("Omar's Orphans") after a wave-off.

it was often unforgiving in carrier landings. Known as the ultimate "day fighter" the F8U-1E version that served on the *Intrepid* when she was an attack carrier had limited all-weather capability. The reconnaissance version, the F8U-1P, also served on the *Intrepid*. Later known as the "MiG master" in Vietnam, it was the last of a long line of fighters to fly from the *Essex*-class carriers with detachments of F-8C fighter and RF-8G reconnaissance variants on the *Intrepid* during her last two deployments as a limited attack carrier off Vietnam.

Tracker, Trader, and Tracer

In the postwar era with the increased threat from Soviet submarines, the Navy developed the twin-engine Grumman S2F Tracker to replace earlier single-engine types that had to be operated in hunter-killer pairs, limiting their usefulness. From the Tracker, the Navy developed the TF-1 Trader as a carrier-based transport and later, the WF Tracer for airborne early warning.

The Grumman S2F Tracker, powered by two 1,525-horsepower Wright R-1820 radial engines, was a large aircraft that was the Navy's first purpose-built carrier antisubmarine aircraft. It could accommodate both search equipment, such as radar and MAD (magnetic anomaly detection) gear, and attack weapons in the form of depth charges and homing torpedoes. Known as the "Stoof," Trackers first deployed with squadrons in early 1954 and were larger than any other carrier aircraft at the time except the AJ-1 Savage. The Tracker was redesignated as the S-2 and served on antisubmarine warfare carriers until the 1970s.

Tracker preparing to launch in November 1969.

C-1 Traders
prepared to launch
off *Intrepid*, 1958.

The Grumman TF Trader was a development of the Tracker to provide carrier onboard delivery (COD) services to carriers at sea. The COD concept was developed during the Korean War with modified Grumman Avengers to ferry personnel, supplies, and high-priority cargo, such as replacement parts, from shore bases to an aircraft carrier at sea and the Trader proved to be a vast improvement. It was outfitted to carry nine passengers or 3,500 pounds of cargo and first flew in 1955. Perhaps the most important cargo, from a sailor's point of view, was mail. The COD delivered mail to carriers serving on station, particularly during the Vietnam War. The Trader would become the last piston-engine aircraft in Navy service, the last being withdrawn in 1988.

The Grumman WF Tracer was the Navy's first purpose-built carrier airborne early warning aircraft. With the continuous improvements in early airborne radars, the Navy decided in 1956 to develop an airborne early warning and command-and-control aircraft. Tracer, a derivative of the Trader, entered service in 1958, replacing the Skyraider early warning variants. Its most distinctive feature was the large aerodynamically shaped radome that housed the APS-82 radar. This radar had many new features for the time, such as a stabilized antenna and an airborne moving target indicator capability that allowed the radar to detect low flying targets against the clutter of radar reflections from the ocean. Originally known as the "Willy Fudd" or the "Stoof with a Roof" because of its large radome, the Tracer was redesignated as the E-1 in 1962. It would be replaced on larger carriers by the Grumman E-2 Hawkeye but would serve into the 1970s on the *Essex*-class ships.

A Tracer from VAW-112
preparing to launch in the
Gulf of Tonkin, 1968.

ASW CARRIER

AS THE THREAT FROM SOVIET SUBMARINES GREW AFTER THE KOREAN
War, the Navy decided to create specialized antisubmarine warfare (ASW) support carriers, CVS, and older *Essex*-class carriers that had not been modernized assumed the ASW role. As new carriers of the *Forrestal* class and later classes entered service, more *Essex*-class carriers were converted to ASW carriers and those ships that had been modernized under the SCB-27A program in turn replaced their un-modernized sisters. On 10 March 1962, the *Intrepid* entered the Norfolk Navy Yard in Portsmouth, Virginia, for overhaul and refitting as an ASW carrier and was redesignated CVS-11 on 31 March 1962. She would be the only SCB-27C ship to be so converted, and her C-11 steam catapults would later allow her to serve in the Vietnam War as a limited attack carrier.

Intrepid steams up the Hudson River as her crew and 243 members of the American Institute of Aeronautics and Astronautics salute New York with "hi N.Y.C." during her visit from 17 to 19 May 1962.

After leaving Portsmouth early in April, the *Intrepid* embarked Antisubmarine Carrier Air Group 56 (CVSG-56) and began a few days of carrier qualifications (carquals) in the Virginia Capes to familiarize her new squadrons with the *Intrepid*. Later she departed for Puerto Rico, staying briefly before proceeding to Guantanamo Bay, conducting more carquals enroute. After a brief stay, she returned to Norfolk on 8 May as a fully qualified ASW carrier. CVSG-56 included two fixed-wing antisubmarine squadrons, VS-24 and V-27, flying the S2F Tracker and an antisubmarine helicopter squadron, HS-3, equipped with HSS-2 Sea King helicopters. A VAW-33 detachment with AD-5W Skyraiders performed airborne early warning. Typically, a CVS would operate with eight destroyers, four to provide a screen around the carrier and four to prosecute distant contacts. Trackers would be on station to monitor sonobuoy searches and Sea Kings would provide continuous coverage of contacts, while the Skyraiders provided electronic warfare support. In 1962 these aircraft were redesignated under the new unified system, the S2F becoming the S-2, the HSS becoming the SH-3, and the AD-5W becoming the EA-1. During the *Intrepid*'s next at sea period she played a part in a historic event.

In the early days of the space program Navy ships were often called upon to recover capsules on their return to earth. The *Intrepid* was selected to be the prime recovery ship for America's fourth manned space flight, the Aurora 7, piloted by Lieutenant Commander Scott Carpenter. One of the original seven Mercury astronauts, Carpenter became the second American to orbit the earth a few months after John Glenn's historic flight. On 24 May 1962, the Aurora 7 capsule was launched from Cape Canaveral atop an Atlas rocket and, after completing three orbits, the Aurora 7 overshot the landing target by about 250 miles. Fortunately, Navy P2V Neptune patrol planes were able to pick up the capsule's homing beacon and reached the scene nearly an hour after splashdown. There they found Carpenter alongside his floating capsule, waving from a raft dropped by an Air Force air-sea rescue aircraft. Two Sea Kings from HS-3 were sent from the *Intrepid*, one would pick up the astronaut while the other put two divers in the water to assist in attaching a floatation device to the capsule. Carpenter told the helo crew that he was short on flight hours for the

previous two months and the hour logged on the return to the *Intrepid* would add to the five hours he logged in the Aurora 7, putting him over the requirement. Once Carpenter was on board the *Intrepid*, Captain Abbot presented him with a ship's plaque, and he shared a meal with the captain and other senior officers before being flown back to the states that evening. The *Intrepid*, having done her part, returned to Norfolk on 31 May.

While at Norfolk, Captain Robert J. Morgan relieved Captain Abbot on 14 June. On 6 July, the *Intrepid* left Norfolk and headed for Quebec City with more than 200 midshipmen from 15 universities and colleges on board. During the next two weeks of steaming she sharpened her antisubmarine warfare skills and arrived on 20 July. The *Intrepid* sailors enjoyed the friendliness of the local citizens who visited the ship by the thousands. Departing on 27 July, the *Intrepid* arrived back at Norfolk on 5 August when the midshipmen departed. She would spend another few weeks operating in the Virginia Capes before heading to Portsmouth for her first major

Scott Carpenter is picked up by an SH-3 from HS-3 while his Aurora 7 space capsule floats nearby, 24 May 1962.

overhaul since 1959. From September to December 1962 her hull was chipped, primed, and painted while the flight deck received a new coat of teakwood and six of her eight boilers were re-bricked. The galley was updated and other repairs were made. By the end of December, the work was complete and she left Norfolk on 23 January 1963 and headed to Guantanamo Bay for refresher training. In February she visited Kingston, Jamaica, for a three-day port call. Her training was interrupted, however, to respond to an international terrorist incident. On 12 February 1963, nine leftist extremists hijacked the Venezuelan freighter SS *Anzoategui* 60 miles off the coast, taking the crew hostage.

Scott Carpenter is welcomed on board *Intrepid* after his recovery.

The government in Caracas called for international aid in recapturing the vessel and the *Intrepid* joined in the search efforts. An American patrol aircraft spotted the ship, which eventually reached Belem, Brazil, where the hijackers turned themselves in and were taken into custody. Some were later allowed to fly to Cuba, while others asked for asylum in Brazil.

From March to May, the *Intrepid* was tied up at Norfolk Naval Base. On 20 April, Captain Morgan was relieved by Captain John C. Lawrence, who had been squadron commander of VT-10 on board the *Intrepid* during World War II. Throughout 1963, the *Intrepid* continued to operate locally in the Atlantic and the Caribbean

with CVSG-56. Interspersed with midshipmen summer cruises were port visits to various cities, including New York in May for a cruise for members of the American Institute of Aeronautics and Astronautics (AIAA) as well as participation in the annual Armed Forces Day parade. The rest of 1963 was taken up with exercises and port calls to Hamilton, Bermuda; Halifax, Nova Scotia; Boston; and Quebec.

After spending the holidays in port at Norfolk, the *Intrepid* got underway 13 January 1964 and headed for the Caribbean, where she would participate in Operation Springboard, an annual program of basic and inter-type training exercises interspersed with visits to Puerto Rico, the U.S. Virgin Islands, and the British West Indies. In March, while operating in the Virginia Capes, NASA officials came aboard to gather information on recovery techniques for the upcoming Gemini and Apollo space programs as well as conduct practice recoveries.

Captain Joseph G. Smith, who had at one time been an Army Second Lieutenant and, as a PBY Catalina pilot, was credited with the first sighting of the Japanese fleet during the battle of the Coral Sea in World War II, assumed command from Captain Lawrence on 30 April 1964. In June, the *Intrepid* departed for operations in the Mediterranean that would combine ASW exercises

View of *Intrepid* underway in the Mediterranean Sea, circa 1964.

with midshipmen training before returning to Norfolk in September. For the rest of the year and into the next she would continue to operate in the Western Atlantic and Caribbean. For her at-sea period in the Western Atlantic from November to December 1964 she embarked CVSG-58 with VS-26, VS-36, and HS-7. A detachment from VAW-12 flew the Grumman E-1 Tracer, marking the first time that this aircraft operated from the *Intrepid*. (The Tracer, previously designated WF, was the Navy's first purpose-built carrier airborne early warning aircraft.) During a brief deployment off the North Carolina coast on the night of 21 November, an aircraft tow tractor skidded out of control into the starboard catwalk, sending its driver into the choppy Atlantic, but prompt rescue efforts had the sailor back on board by helo in only 47 minutes.

In March 1965, the *Intrepid* was called on again to serve as prime recovery ship for the space mission Gemini III, the first manned mission in NASA's Gemini program, which followed the original Mercury series of manned space flights and was the first in which a manned spacecraft performed orbital maneuvers. It would also be the last mission to be controlled from Cape Kennedy before NASA shifted to the new Manned Spacecraft Center in Houston, Texas. On 23 March 1965, a Titan II rocket launched astronauts Major Virgil I. "Gus" Grissom and Lieutenant Commander John W. Young into space. After completing three low-earth orbits, their capsule, the Molly Brown, splashed down northeast of Grand Turk Island about 50 miles short of the projected landing point in an otherwise flawless flight. The original plan called for the crew to remain on board until the capsule was recovered, but since the *Intrepid* was further away, Grissom requested to be picked up by helicopter. Remembering his loss of the Liberty Bell 7 on the second Mercury flight, he would not open the hatch until Navy divers had attached the floatation collar to the "unsinkable" Molly Brown. Within an hour both astronauts stepped aboard the *Intrepid*. (NASA had not been happy with the name Grissom had chosen for

Antisubmarine Warfare Carriers

As the carrier force entered the 1960s, air groups changed to reflect new missions and capabilities. Antisubmarine carrier air groups (CVSG) were established in 1960–1961 and given numbers between 50 and 60. These antisubmarine air groups continued to be called air groups even after the attack carrier air groups were re-titled as wings (CVW) in 1963. An antisubmarine air group included two VS fixed-wing antisubmarine squadrons flying the S-2 Tracker, an HS helicopter antisubmarine squadron equipped with SH-3 Sea King helicopters, and a VAW airborne early warning squadron with E-1 Tracers. Operating in the Pacific and Atlantic, the antisubmarine carriers monitored the growing Soviet submarine force, and, as ASW gained in importance, the ships were modernized under an overall Navy effort known as the Fleet Rehabilitation and Modernization II program. SCB-144 was the FRAM II modernization aimed at improving the ASW capabilities of the SCB-27A CVS carriers. By 1965 all the FRAM II conversions were back in service.

As American involvement in Vietnam grew, the antisubmarine carriers of the Pacific Fleet performed the vital, if less conspicuous, role of providing ASW protection for the naval forces in the South China Sea. In addition to antisubmarine screening, they performed surface surveillance and combat search and rescue missions. Occasionally, their detachments of A-4 Skyhawk "fighters" were used to launch strikes at ground targets. During the peak years of 1964 through 1969, the *Yorktown*, *Hornet*, *Bennington*, and *Kearsarge* rotated through deployments to Vietnam. The ASW carriers responded to other hot spots in the Pacific as well. The *Yorktown*, on her way to South Vietnam, was diverted to the Sea of Japan following the seizure of the spy ship Pueblo off Wonsan, North Korea, on 28 January 1968. She maintained a readiness patrol for 48 days before being released to continue her deployment. Trouble with North Korea flared again the next year. In April 1969, the *Hornet*, nearing the end of her deployment to the Western Pacific, was diverted to the Sea of Japan when a Navy reconnaissance aircraft was shot down. She remained in the area for two weeks before continuing to Long Beach. The *Intrepid*, as an Atlantic Fleet antisubmarine carrier, was loaned to the war effort as a "special attack carrier" and completed three combat deployments, though she retained her CVS designation.

A frogman is lowered to the Gemini III spacecraft from an SH-3 from helicopter squadron HS-3, 23 March 1965.

Frogmen secure the floatation collar to the "unsinkable" Molly Brown space capsule.

The Molly Brown space capsule is hoisted onto *Intrepid*, 23 March 1965.

John Young (left) and Gus Grissom pose for photographers with their space capsule.

the capsule, Molly Brown having been a survivor of the *Titanic* and the subject of a Hollywood movie starring Debbie Reynolds. John Young had created his own small scandal by smuggling a corned beef sandwich aboard in the pocket of his space suit.)

In the late 1950s, many of the Navy's ships built during World War II were wearing out, and the service initiated the Fleet Rehabilitation and Modernization program to extend the active service life of these ships. Faced with the rising costs of the Vietnam War, the CVS carriers were part of a more austere version, FRAM II. Most of the SCB-27A CVS carriers came under this program and the *Intrepid* would be the only SCB 27C carrier to be so modernized. The *Intrepid* underwent her FRAM II modernization at the New York Naval

Shipyard in Brooklyn from April to September 1965. After off-loading ammunition and excess fuel, the *Intrepid* stopped at Bayonne, New Jersey, to have her topside radar antennas and pole mast removed to allow her to pass under the Brooklyn Bridge. She pulled into the Brooklyn Navy Yard on 16 April for her $10 million overhaul—the last major repair job performed there before its closing. While in port, Captain Giuseppi "Gus" Macri, who had been a torpedo bomber squadron skipper in World War II, replaced Captain Smith on 13 May. After her work was competed, the *Intrepid* got underway for Norfolk and arrived on 16 October. After local operations in November, the *Intrepid* began preparations for her deployment to Vietnam as "limited attack carrier."

The dome for the bow-mounted SQS-23 sonar awaiting installation on the hull of *Intrepid*. The inscription reads, "Brooklyn Navy Yard Makes Its Final Bow," a witty comment on the closing of the Navy Yard.

(below) A view of the changes to *Intrepid*'s bow with the new sonar dome and stem-mounted anchor.

FRAM II

The Navy's Fleet Rehabilitation and Modernization program extended the lives of World War II–era ships by improving their antisubmarine warfare capabilities against the growing Soviet submarine threat. It covered destroyers, cruisers, aircraft carriers, submarines, amphibious ships, and auxiliaries. The *Intrepid*'s FRAM II modernization added a bow-mounted SQS-23 sonar, new tactical displays in the combat information center, new electronic counter-measure equipment, and a new tactical data link that would permit the exchange of data with APS-82 radar on the E-1 Tracer carrier airborne early warning aircraft. Repairs included flight deck planking, re-bricking and re-tubing of boilers, hull reinforcement, improvements to the catapults and arresting gear, re-cabling of aircraft elevators, and renovation of the 5-inch gun mounts. Besides the bow mounted sonar, new additions included a Fresnel lens landing system to replace the previous mirror landing system, a Pilot Landing Aid Television (PLAT), and new electronic and gear and other equipment. The port anchor was replaced by a centerline anchor with a stem hawse pipe to clear the bow sonar.

VIETNAM

THE *INTREPID* LEFT NORFOLK IN EARLY NOVEMBER 1965 FOR GUANTANAMO Bay and a five-week refresher training cruise with training concentrated on the attack carrier role instead of antisubmarine warfare. After spending Thanksgiving in Kingston, Jamaica, the *Intrepid* headed home, where she began five weeks of restricted availability at Portsmouth for repairs. She departed on 1 February 1966 with Air Wing 10, which had previously been associated with the attack carrier *Shangri-La* and came aboard the following day for more training. On 23 February, Secretary of Defense Robert S. McNamara announced the decision to send the *Intrepid* to Vietnam, stating "In order to maintain the attack carrier force off Vietnam, we are, as I noted, deploying one of the Atlantic-based carriers, the *Intrepid*, to Southeast Asia. Very minor modifications were required on this vessel to permit it to operate light attack aircraft, and it can be quickly reassigned to its antisubmarine role. What is involved is mainly a change in aircraft complement.

Intrepid in Kingston Harbor, Jamaica, during five weeks of refresher training in the Caribbean, November 1965. The aircraft on her flight deck, Skyhawks and Skyraiders, reflect her preparations as a limited attack carrier before her deployment to Vietnam.

The antisubmarine air group is being retained in the active fleet, thus giving us the capability to operate the carrier as a CVS on short notice."

The day before the official announcement however, the *Intrepid* suffered minor damage in a collision with the oiler *Sabine* (AO-25) during refueling off the coast of Florida. While alongside, a steering casualty on the *Sabine* caused her to veer sharply to port, hitting the *Intrepid* amidships on the starboard side. Part of a sponson was ripped away and several fuel tanks were ruptured. Returning to the Norfolk Naval

During an underway replenishment with the *Mauna Loa* (AE-8), *Intrepid* receives a load of rocket motors, 17 February 1966.

Shipyard, repairs were completed by 18 March and there was no delay in her deployment. She put to sea again and conducted six days of operational training with her new air wing. CVW-10 was unique in that it was an all attack air wing composed of two squadrons from the East Coast—VA-15, an A-4 Skyhawk squadron from Naval Air Station Cecil, and VA-176 flying A-1 Skyraiders from NAS Jacksonville. There were also two from the West Coast—VA-95 with A-4s from NAS Lemoore and VA-165 with A-1s from NAS Alameda, along with a detachment that had been assigned to CVSG-56, VAW-33 Det. 11 with the EA-1, and a contingent of rescue and utility helicopters from HC-2 Det. 11 with the UH-2A. Both VA-165 and VA-95, as West Coast squadrons with previous deployments to Southeast Asia, brought a wealth of combat experience to the air wing.

After another short yard period to correct a minor problem with a steam turbine, the *Intrepid* departed from Norfolk on 4 April, crossing the Atlantic and entering the Mediterranean, where she spent two days in Naples, Italy, before

continuing east to the Suez Canal. Early in the morning of 23 April, the *Intrepid* began her transit into the Indian Ocean, which she entered on 26 April. By 4 May she had entered the South China Sea and after a brief stay from 7 to 12 May at Subic Bay in the Philippines to make final preparations, she headed for Dixie Station. These were the same waters that she had operated in during World War II with the same Carrier Air Wing 10 that at

Intrepid refueling the destroyer *Borie* (DD-704), 20 February 1966.

Vietnam Region

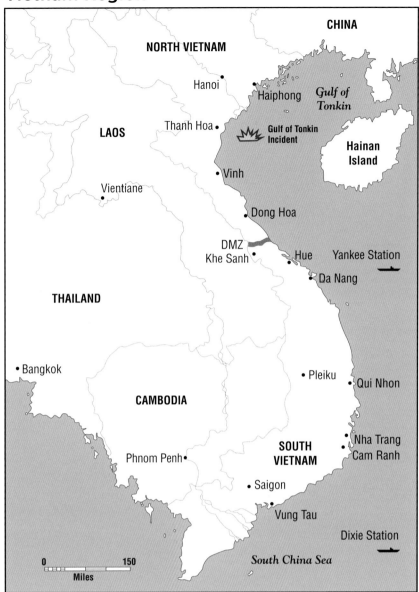

the time was commanded by the same man, Vice Admiral John J. Hyland, who now commanded the Seventh Fleet. Starting on 15 May, she began 31 days of operations providing in-country support while steaming about 60 miles off the Mekong Delta. Air Wing 10 flew a total of 2,412 sorties during this line period, earning the praise of General Westmoreland, commander of all the ground forces in Vietnam. Interspersed with air operations the *Intrepid* also conducted underway replenishments to take on aviation gasoline, JP-5 jet fuel, fuel oil, ammunition, and various stores. She also provided fuel oil to her escorting destroyers. Refueling usually took place early in the morning so that the final break-away could be completed before the beginning of the first launch. Rearming was usually done in the late morning, often requiring the *Intrepid* to break away and turn into the wind to launch aircraft. Upon completion of her first line period on 15 June, the *Intrepid* left Dixie Station and headed for Yokosuka, Japan.

A UH-2 from HC-2 Detachment 11 during *Intrepid*'s second Vietnam deployment in 1967.

Seasprite

The Kaman UH-2 Seasprite was originally developed as an ASW and utility helicopter capable of operating from smaller warships. The UH-2A and UH-2B versions operated off the *Intrepid* during her Vietnam deployments. These helicopters had a single 1,250-shaft horsepower General Electric T58 engine, with later versions having two engines.

After completing her first combat period without a mishap, the *Intrepid* had its first aviation accident on the night of 19 June. At about 2200 a man overboard was reported and a UH-2A helicopter was quickly launched to attempt a rescue but crashed almost immediately after takeoff. A boat was put in the water but could only find one badly injured survivor from the four-man crew. Unfortunately, a muster soon revealed that the man overboard call had been a mistake on the part of a lookout. After a futile search for the rest of the helicopter crew, the *Intrepid* continued to Yokosuka, arriving on 21 June for 10 days of rest and recreation.

An A-4B preparing to launch for air strikes over Vietnam, 20 May 1966.

After departing Yokosuka 1 July, the *Intrepid* arrived on Dixie Station on the 8th. During her second line period, Captain John W. Fair relieved Captain Macri on 15 July. The *Intrepid* stayed on Dixie Station until 4 August when she headed north to the Gulf of Tonkin to operate on Yankee Station. Arriving two days later, she joined the *Ranger* and *Constellation* for a few days before leaving for Sasebo, Japan, on the 10th. CVW-10 had flown 2,346 sorties during her time on Dixie Station and 294 sorties during her four days on Yankee Station.

The *Intrepid* was in port at Sasebo from 15 to 24 August before departing for a three-day port call at Hong Kong and then arriving at Yankee Station on 1 September. While on Yankee Station, the *Intrepid* took part in coordinated three-carrier attacks on the Thanh Hoa petroleum-oil-lubricant center, rail facilities, power plants, and the Ninh Binh rail and ship repair facilities. The *Intrepid* left the line on 23 September and arrived in Subic Bay two days later. After six days at Subic, she departed for her final line period of the deployment on Yankee Station from 2 to 18 October.

Of note during this deployment was the second aerial kill of a MiG by a propeller-driven Skyraider. (The first had been a MiG-17 shot down by VA-25 off the *Midway* on 20 June 1965.) On 9 October 1966, a flight from VA-176 led by Lieutenant Commander Leo Cook with Lieutenant Junior Grade James W. "Jim" Wiley

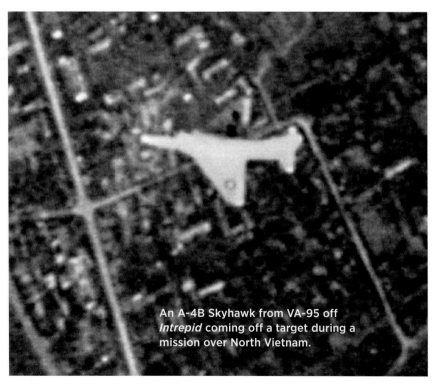

An A-4B Skyhawk from VA-95 off *Intrepid* coming off a target during a mission over North Vietnam.

as his wingman and a second section led by Lieutenant Peter "Pete" Russell with Lieutenant Junior Grade William T. "Tom" Patton as his wingman, was launched from the *Intrepid* on a rescue combat air patrol mission supporting strikes over North Vietnam. While searching for the pilot of a downed F-4 from another carrier, the flight was jumped by four MiG-17s and during the action that followed Patton gained a good position on one of the MiGs and opened fire with his four cannons, hitting the MiG's tail. Patton followed the MiG down through the clouds and when he broke into the clear he spotted the enemy pilot's parachute. Patton was given credit for a kill and Wiley was credited with a possible kill after scoring 20-mm hits on one of the MiGs, which was seen trailing smoke as it left the area, while a third was heavily damaged.

Bad weather continued to hamper operations during this last line period as the monsoon season reached its peak over North Vietnam. A total of 845 sorties were flown before the *Intrepid* left the line on 18 October. After a few days at Cubi Point, the *Intrepid* began the long journey home on 25

Planes strike the railway facilities at Minh Binh during a four-day attack on North Vietnamese railway transport there, 18 September 1966.

Lieutenant (j.g.) William T. Patton of VA-176 describes how he shot down a North Vietnamese MiG-17 with his A-1H Skyraider during a mission over North Vietnam, 10 October 1966.

October. A highlight of the return was the crossing of the equator on 27 October during which, by longstanding seafaring tradition, shellbacks (those who have crossed the equator) initiate polywogs (those who have not) in ceremonies that trace their origins to the days of sail.

Retracing her course through the Indian Ocean into the Suez Canal, the *Intrepid* proceeded through the Mediterranean and into the Atlantic, arriving in Mayport, Florida, on 21 November to offload CVW-10

before proceeding to the Norfolk Naval Station, heavy weather delaying her return until the 23rd. She moved to the naval shipyard on the 30th and entered drydock on 10 December. After minor repairs, alterations, and modifications, she left on 4 March 1967 for three days of post-repair sea trials off the Virginia Capes before returning to the naval station for two weeks of maintenance and upkeep in preparation for her next deployment to Vietnam.

This A-1H Skyraider, as seen at Naval Air Station (NAS) Quonset Point, Rhode Island, on 5 June 1967 is the one flown by Lieutenant (j.g.) Patton for his MiG kill on 9 October 1966.

ANOTHER TOUR

ON 13 MARCH 1967 THE *INTREPID* LEFT NORFOLK FOR THE VIRGINIA Capes to begin working up for her next deployment to Vietnam with Air Wing 10. This time CVW-10 consisted of three Skyhawk squadrons, a Skyraider squadron, and several detachments. The A-4 squadrons were VA-15, VA-34, and VSF-3. Anti-Submarine Fighter Squadrons (VSF) were originally intended to provide some defensive

An RF-8G of VFP-63 Det. 11, the "Eyes of the Fleet," tied down forward of the island.

capability for the CVS carriers. When the original VSF-1 became too large it was split in two, VSF-1 for the Atlantic and VSF-3 for the Pacific. The VSF squadrons were really attack squadrons in all but name. The real fighter protection was from the F-8 Crusaders of VF-111 Det. 11 "Omar's Orphans" while the other Crusader detachment, VFP-63 Det. 11 had photo

to do so before it closed with the outbreak of war between Israel and the Arab states.

The transit was not without incident. On 14 June, the day before *Intrepid* pulled into Subic Bay, a UH-2 helicopter was lost due to an operational difficulty, although all four of the crew were soon picked up by another UH-2. After completing final preparations at

Skyhawks of VSF-3 in flight during Intrepid's second Vietnam cruise. For all intents, VSF-3 was just another attack squadron, although it did fly the older A-4B version compared to the A-4Cs of her sister squadrons, VA-15 and VA-34.

reconnaissance RF-8s. The Skyraider squadron was VA-145, while VAW-33 Det. 11 performed electronic warfare with the EA-1. VAW-121 Det. 11 flew the airborne early warning E-1 Tracer and HC-2 Det. 11 performed utility and rescue work with the UH-2 Seasprite helicopter. She returned for upkeep and maintenance on 25 March after completing carrier qualifications. After having completed various readiness drills and inspections, the *Intrepid*, with CVW-10 on board, departed for her second deployment to Vietnam. Again she crossed the Atlantic and entered the Mediterranean, but her passage through the Suez Canal was delayed due to mounting Arab-Israeli tensions. From the last day of May to the first day of June 1967, the *Intrepid* at last sailed through the Suez Canal, the last American warship

An A-4C from the VA-34 "Blue Blasters" being directed into position for launch.

Subic Bay, the *Intrepid* departed on 19 June, arriving on Yankee Station two days later. For the next six months she would strike various targets in North Vietnam. During her first line period CVW-10 heavily damaged the Ben Thuy power plant and the petroleum products storage areas at Haiphong and Don Son, while also hitting railroad sidings and yards, as well as destroying the Ban Yen Nhan army barracks. Altogether 1,732 sorties were flown during the 23 days of her first line period. As during her first Vietnam deployment, underway replenishments were conducted every few days to refuel and rearm. On 26 June Captain William J. McVey relieved Captain Fair in a ceremony on the flight deck. From 13 to 16 July, the *Intrepid* sailed to Yokosuka, Japan, where she entered drydock on arrival to replace two propellers that had been damaged during her transit

An A-4 takes the barrier on *Intrepid* in the Gulf of Tonkin, 1 July 1967.

The Haiphong Highway bridge is attacked by planes from *Intrepid*, October 1967.

UNITED STATES NAVAL INSTITUTE

Since the RF-8s of VFP-63 were unarmed, post-strike reconnaissance missions would require escort by VF-111.

to the Pacific. Taking advantage of the extended stay, many *Intrepid* sailors took the opportunity to visit Japanese cities and other points of interest. Departing for Vietnam on 25 July, the *Intrepid* was ordered to assist the carrier *Forrestal* while still en route. Fire had broken out on board the *Forrestal* on the morning of 29 July and when the *Intrepid* arrived, she was still smoldering. Fire fighting foam was transported to the *Forrestal* by helicopter while a medical team was sent to the *Oriskany* to help treat the *Forrestal* casualties. Blood and stretchers were also transferred to the hospital ship *Repose*. She also hosted newsmen and VIPs who had arrived on the scene.

By afternoon the next day, the *Intrepid*'s second line period began with strikes against targets in North Vietnam. Four railroad/highway bridges were destroyed and another heavily damaged, while a main highway bridge was destroyed and another heavily damaged. Two barracks areas were destroyed and buildings on Kien An airfield were damaged. At the Port Wallut Naval Base along the border with China, buildings, piers, and torpedo boats were hit. During the 29 days

on the line, CVW-10 flew 1,651 combat sorties and 615 combat support sorties. On a lighter note, a USO show featured Miss America, Jane Anne Jayroe, and her court performing "What's Happening Back Home" for the crew on 21 August. The visit also served as an opportunity to celebrate the *Intrepid*'s 24th birthday and a 1,400-pound cake was prepared for the occasion.

The *Intrepid* left Yankee Station on 27 August for Subic Bay, where she stayed from 29 to 31 August before heading for Hong Kong. She arrived there on 1 September for five days of rest and relaxation before heading back to Subic Bay. After a brief stay, she was back on the line by 15 September for her third line period. Although the monsoon weather again limited air operations as on her first deployment the year before, CVW-10 still flew 1,152 combat sorties and 539 combat support sorties during the 28 days on the line despite losing seven flying days due to the weather. Eight important bridges and ferries were seeded with electronic sensors, the Kien An and Haiphong highway bridges were destroyed, and two power plants were heavily damaged.

An F-8C of VF-111 "Omar's Orphans" takes a bolter off the angle. The Crusader took a cat shot easily, but could be tricky trapping aboard.

Intrepid underway in the Gulf of Tonkin, 1967.

On 12 October, the *Intrepid* headed again for Yokosuka and arrived on the 17th. Her departure was delayed for 48 hours until the 26th due to the threat of Typhoon Dinah, which at the time was 100 miles south of Okinawa. She encountered high winds and heavy seas as she skirted 200 miles to the south of the storm and did not arrive on Yankee Station for her fourth and final line period until 1 November. The day after her arrival, a lifting cable on the after starboard elevator platform parted from exposure and use, requiring the elevator to be raised to the flight deck and locked in the up position. It remained that way for the rest of the line period, but flight operations continued. On 5 November, the *Intrepid, Constellation, Oriskany,* and other units of the Seventh Fleet were forced to evade Typhoon Emma, then about 400 miles southeast of the Gulf of Tonkin. The storm passed over Hainan Island on 7 November and combat operations resumed the next day. Bridges were hit hard in *Intrepid*'s last line period—51 were destroyed or damaged, including seven bypass bridges destroyed. CVW-10 destroyed or damaged 693 supply boats and 44 railroad cars and damaged support at Haiphong's Kien An airfield. All this was accomplished by 1,206 combat sorties during the 24 days on the line, with four days lost to weather. The *Intrepid* left Yankee Station on 24 November and headed for Subic Bay. Twelve aircraft had been lost during her time on station. Of the six pilots lost, in four cases their aircraft were hit by flak and two by surface-to-air missiles (SAM). Three of the six pilots lost were listed as missing in action and the other three as prisoners of war. Of the other six aircraft lost, one was brought down by a SAM and three were lost to flak during major strikes while the other two were downed by flak during armed reconnaissance missions. Six pilots were rescued; five made it to the Gulf of Tonkin and were quickly rescued by helicopter, but the sixth had landed only a mile from Haiphong Harbor in water that was only two feet deep, providing for an exciting rescue. After the *Intrepid* left Yankee Station, another aircraft, an A-4 flying from Cubi Point Naval Air Station, was lost on 26 November when its engine flamed out. The pilot ejected however and was quickly rescued.

The *Intrepid* put on a unique USO show during this period. Her band, the "Oceanaires," was launched from *Intrepid* on 12 November from Yankee Station for a 10-day tour of South Vietnam, with 90-minute variety show performances at Chu Lai, Pleiku, An Khe, Phan Rang, Cam Ranh Bay, Cat Lai, and Saigon. Martha Raye even asked the band to stay on with her own USO show, but this was not possible given the ship's schedule. This was the first time a Navy band ever performed on the USO circuit in Vietnam.

Upon arriving at Subic Bay on 27 November, the *Intrepid* spent four days offloading ordnance and loading supplies for the return to Norfolk. On her return voyage she rounded the southern tip of Africa via the Cape of Good Hope and into the South Atlantic, celebrating Christmas at sea before finally docking in Norfolk on 30 December. In the first few days of 1968, all remaining aircraft and ordnance were offloaded before the *Intrepid* entered the Norfolk Navy Yard for a period of restricted availability.

Family and friends board *Intrepid* after her return to Norfolk at the end of December 1967.

A THIRD TIME AROUND

AFTER RETURNING FROM HER SECOND CONSECUTIVE VIETNAM deployment two days before the dawn of the New Year, the *Intrepid* spent the first three months of 1968 undergoing a modified overhaul at the Norfolk Naval Shipyard. While being scraped and repainted, she underwent minor modifications, alterations, and repairs. With her overhaul complete, she got underway in early March for a brief five-day cruise. After shakedown and training exercises, the *Intrepid* departed Norfolk on 4 June for her third Vietnam cruise. Her course would take her south. After a brief stop at St. Thomas, in the U.S. Virgin Islands, the *Intrepid* arrived at Rio de Janeiro, Brazil, on 22 June for a two-day

Families and friends of the *Intrepid* crew gather on the pier at Naval Station (NS) Norfolk, Virginia, as the ship departs for Vietnam. Moored nearby is the *Forrestal* (CVA-59), 4 June 1968.

UNITED STATES NAVAL INSTITUTE

port call. While in port on the first day, in a completely different setting from the year before when Captain McVey assumed command while the *Intrepid* was on the line in the Tonkin Gulf, Captain Vincent F. Kelley assumed command. Except for a brief period from November to December 1968 when he was hospitalized for an abdominal operation and Captain Whitney Wright took over as acting commander, he remained in command until August 1969.

After departing Rio, the *Intrepid* crossed the South Atlantic, rounding the Cape of Good Hope into the Indian Ocean, and arrived at Subic Bay in the Philippines on 15 July for six days of final preparations before heading back on the line. On 24 July, she arrived on Yankee Station to begin operations

Yard workers measure new lumber to replace the old in drydock at Philadelphia Naval Shipyard, 19 March 1968

with Air Wing 10, which now had A-4 squadrons VA-36, VA-66, and VA-106, and VAW-33 had become VAQ-33. Their goal was interdiction operations against enemy supply routes in the southern area.

The A-4s of CVW-10 struck bridges, transshipment points, and storage areas and rendered many highways and logistics targets unserviceable. In a coordinated multi-carrier strike in the Vinh area on

Unloading bombs from shipping pallets to bomb carts for easier transport through tight spaces on board the ship, 27 July 1968. Replenishing fuel and munitions was a continuing cycle while operating off Vietnam.

1 August, the *Intrepid* Skyhawks inflicted heavy damage in the Ru Muon military installation. Elsewhere, a section of the *Intrepid*'s F-8 aircraft from VF-111 teamed up with F-8s from the *Bon Homme Richard* (CV-31) to bring down a MiG-21 but success was not without its price. On the same day, an A-4C from VA-66 was lost due to unknown causes during a mission over Dong Dun transshipment point.

During the first line period of 50 days, the *Intrepid*'s aviators flew a total of 1,781 combat sorties, 421 combat support sorties, 54 photo missions, and 82 RESCAP missions. At the conclusion of this tour, she left Yankee Station for Sasebo, Japan, for a

period of routine upkeep and rest and recreation from 26 August through 1 September.

On 5 September, she was back on Yankee Station and, following Tropical Storm Bess, her A-4s took to the air again. In three large-scale coordinated strikes in the Vinh Son area, the *Intrepid* aircraft destroyed a SAM site, the Vinh Son Headquarters of the 524th Infantry Division, and inflicted heavy damage in the Yen Lai truck park. Throughout these missions, the aircraft had to fly through barrages of 37-mm and 57-mm antiaircraft fire to get to their targets. During the remainder of the line period, the carrier's aircraft destroyed 8 bridges, 80 small vessels used to transport supplies (referred to as waterborne logistics craft), and 20 trucks.

On 19 September 1968, two F-8s were launched from the *Intrepid* on an intercept mission. The section leader, Lieutenant Anthony J. Nargi, spotted a bogie that he closed on and identified as a MiG-21. "I think he saw me about the same time," he noted later. The MiG attempted to evade him by executing a loop, but Nargi closed the distance and launched a Sidewinder missile from a near perfect position astern and saw the missile fly up the MiG's tailpipe and explode, separating the tail of the MiG as the fuselage was engulfed in a red fireball. The pilot was seen to eject, but Nargi and his wingman Lieutenant (j.g.) Alexander Rucker, turned their attention to another MiG. Both fired missiles at the second MiG, which detonated near it, but it escaped to the north. Back on board the *Intrepid*, Nargi talked about his lucky number. He was flying from VF-111 on his 111th mission from CVS-11. Nargi's kill would be the last Crusader kill of the war before the bombing halt of 1 November.

During a test flight on 23 September, an A-4E from VA-106 struck the landing signal officer platform, killing the pilot and an officer and enlisted man on the platform. When the *Intrepid* ended this second line period, her CVW-10 aircraft had flown 1,216 combat sorties, 314 combat support sorties, and 48 photo reconnaissance missions.

Following periods in Subic Bay and a port call at Hong Kong from 3 to 9 October, the *Intrepid* was back in the Gulf of Tonkin on 15 October and her aircraft began their attacks on enemy supply routes. Their

The deck edge catapult operator receives the signal to "tension" a VA-66 Skyhawk on the starboard catapult during flight operations in the Gulf of Tonkin, September 1968.

An A-4E of the VA-106 Gladiators is brought into launching position on a catapult during flight operations in the Gulf of Tonkin, September 1968. Note the nose wheel steering bar in use.

UNITED STATES NAVAL INSTITUTE

The F-8C flown by Lieutenant Tony Nargi when he shot down a MiG-21 with a Sidewinder missile, 19 September 1968.

Lieutenant Nargi being congratulated by *Intrepid*'s skipper, Captain Kelley.

strikes were successful against bridges, ferries, and river fords, and they destroyed or damaged 26 waterborne logistics craft, 5 barges, 10 trucks, and 4 river ferries. On 21 October, an A-4 from VA-106 was lost when it struck the ground while on a strafing run.

With the announcement of the bombing halt over North Vietnam on 1 November, the *Intrepid* moved south where her aircraft flew missions over South Vietnam and Laos. At the end of her third line period, CVW-10 had flown 1,312 combat sorties, 435 combat support sorties, and 33 photo reconnaissance missions.

After a port call in Singapore from 16 to 22 November and a stop in Subic Bay, the *Intrepid* returned to Yankee Station for her fourth line period on 5 December. Almost all the strikes conducted during this final 22-day line period were against targets in Laos. In all, pilots of CVW-10 flew 1,174 combat sorties, 423 combat support sorties, and 22 photo reconnaissance missions. The *Intrepid* spent Christmas 1968 at sea in the Gulf of Tonkin before she left the line to return to the United States on 27 December 1968. Although CVW-10 was still on board, most of the combat pilots

In the South China Sea, *Intrepid* takes on fuel oil and 500-pound bombs from the fast combat support ship *Camden* (AOE), December 1968.

Crewmen take supplies below by the aft elevator on board *Intrepid* during her underway replenishment (unrep) alongside *Camden*, December 1968.

In addition to underway replenishment (unrep), the Navy has developed vertical replenishment (vertrep). Here UH-46D Sea Knights from *Camden*'s helicopter combat support squadrons HC-3 and HC-7 from combat stores ship *Mars* (AFS-1) bring supplies to *Intrepid*'s flight deck, December 1968.

Intrepid homeward bound from her third Vietnam deployment is refueled as she rounds Cape Horn by the Chilean oiler *Almirante Montt* (AO-52), 25 January 1969. The oiler was alongside for eleven hours to pump enough fuel from her one refueling station.

had left the ship in Subic Bay and had been airlifted out for early reunions with their families.

The return trip across the Pacific included stops at Sydney, Australia, and Wellington, New Zealand. Since the ship had performed well and the crew was proud of the job they had done, the mood on board was contented. The long transit home allowed for a relaxed ship's routine that included periods for sunbathing on the flight deck and sporting events such as boxing, basketball, volleyball, and skeet shooting. After rounding Cape Horn off the tip of South America, she headed for another port call at Rio de Janeiro. The transit to Rio was uneventful except for an underway refueling by the Chilean oiler *Almirante Montt* (AO-52) on 25 January. Impressed by the seamanship of the Chilean sailors, the *Intrepid* passed a message to the *Almirante Montt*: "The well drilled and disciplined deck crews and the most professional performance of the helmsman resulted in the *Intrepid*'s station keeping problems being near zero." After leaving Rio, the *Intrepid* crewmen took part in another line-crossing shellback initiation ceremony before her arrival at Norfolk on 8 February 1969. There the families of her crew could enjoy belated Thanksgiving, Christmas, and New Year's celebrations. On 24 February, she left Norfolk for Philadelphia and a six-month overhaul that began on 27 February with the *Intrepid* in drydock at the Philadelphia Naval Shipyard. On 1 August, Captain Horace N. Moore Jr. relieved Captain Kelley. Overhaul and the training exercises that followed were completed early in September, and on 7 September 1969 she entered her new home port at the Quonset Point Naval Air Station, Rhode Island. On 8 September 1969, the *Intrepid* ran aground off Jamestown, Rhode Island, but was freed after two hours. Between 13 October and 25 November, the *Intrepid* operated out of Guantanamo Bay for operational refresher ASW training with CVSG-52, which included S-2 squadrons, VS-28 and VS-31, the SH-3s of HS-5 and HS-11 Det. 11, and the E-1s of VAW-121 Det. 11. She then returned to home port to close out the year.

THE OLDEST CARRIER

DURING 1970, THE *INTREPID* BECAME THE OLDEST OPERATIONAL fleet carrier in the Navy and continued to perform her vital role as central base and flagship for Commander Antisubmarine Warfare Group Four. (The *Lexington* was older, but as a training carrier [CVT-16], she was technically not part of the active fleet.) Much of the year was spent in carrier qualifications, antisubmarine warfare exercises, and training, operating out of Pensacola and other Florida stations

A Grumman S-2E Tracker antisubmarine plane of VS-31 is hoisted aboard from the pier at Naval Air Station Quonset Point, Rhode Island, 30 September 1969.

and Corpus Christi, Texas. On 1 April 1970 Captain Isham W. Linder relieved Captain Moore. From April to May, the *Intrepid* conducted local operations with CVSG-56 before putting in to the Boston Naval Shipyard for overhaul from 26 May to 22 August. After sea trials, she was back at Quonset Point on 3 September. On 16 September, while doing independent air maneuvers, a T-2C crashed into the sea and both aircraft and pilot were lost. CVSG-56 reported aboard on 22 September and the next day, the *Intrepid* got underway for Halifax, Nova Scotia, and a joint United States–Canadian exercise. A second joint exercise to test the combined ASW group's effectiveness against

Intrepid moored at the pier, Quonset Point, Rhode Island, 17 September 1969.

The catapult officer gives the signal as a Tracker is launched off *Intrepid*, 2 November 1969.

An *Intrepid* sailor peers down at his ship moored at New Orleans, Louisiana, 6 February 1970.

submarine launched ballistic missiles was conducted near Bermuda. During the transit home, the *Intrepid* suffered considerable damage in a storm and went into the Boston Naval Shipyard for repairs on her way home to Quonset Point where she finished out the year with routine upkeep, cleaning, and painting.

The *Intrepid* began 1971 operating out of Quonset Point on carrier qualification and ASW exercises with

CVSG-56 near Bermuda. On 16 April, the *Intrepid* left for a six-month deployment in the Mediterranean and Eastern Atlantic with a detachment of A-4s from VA-45 attached to CVSG-56, which became a standard practice for future deployments. Captain Charles S. Williams Jr. relieved Captain Linder on 30 April. While conducting carrier qualifications and ASW exercises in transit, the *Intrepid* first found herself under surveillance by the Soviets, which would later prove to be considerable. After a port call in Lisbon, Portugal, from 28 April to 2 May, the *Intrepid* took part in a NATO exercise, Rusty Razor, with navies of the United Kingdom, the Netherlands, Portugal, France, Belgium, and West Germany until the 17th. After a port call in Plymouth, England, from 10 to 13 May, the *Intrepid* operated in the eastern end of the Baltic Sea until the 20th, becoming the first U.S. carrier to do so. Soviet surface-, subsurface-, and air-surveillance was considerable. At one point, a Soviet Kamov Ka-25 helicopter even buzzed her flight deck. After a brief port call at Kiel, Germany,

Intrepid returns to Quonset Point, Rhode Island, following a six-month European deployment where she operated in the Mediterranean, Baltic, and Norwegian Seas as well as the Atlantic. Friends, relatives, and well-wishers are on hand to greet her. (Probably after her April to October 1971 deployment.)

the *Intrepid* proceeded through the English Channel and sailed through the Straits of Gibraltar into the Mediterranean at the end of the month. While there she made port calls at Naples, Italy; Cannes, France; and Barcelona, Spain. July found the *Intrepid* making port calls in Hamburg, Germany, and Copenhagen, Denmark. On 30 July, on her way to Greenock, Scotland, one of her SH-3 helicopters crashed at sea while attempting a landing, but the crew was rescued as Soviet vessels looked on at a distance. On 12 August, the *Intrepid* was overflown by two Tupolev

Tu-95 Bear bombers as she conducted ASW exercises in the Norwegian Sea from 11th to the 17th. After a brief in-port visit in Rosyth, Scotland, the *Intrepid* got underway for the Norwegian Sea and the Arctic Circle for exercise Alert Lancer. In port at Portsmouth, England, in September she proceeded to Bergen, Norway, conducting exercise Agile Warrior en route. Visiting Bergen from the 22nd through the 25th, she participated in NATO exercise Royal Knight on her way back to Greenock for a brief stay before leaving for Quonset Point. On 15 October, she returned home

A-4E Skyhawk of VA-45 Det. 1 escorts a Soviet Naval Air Force Tu-16 Badger reconnaissance aircraft, circa the 1970s. (VA-45 Det. 1 was assigned to CVSG-56 during the July to October 1972 NorLant cruise and the November 1972–May 1973 NorLant, Med cruise.)

Intrepid underway in the early 1970s with aircraft of CVSG-56 on deck. Visible are S-2 Trackers, E-1B Tracers, and an SH-3D Sea King helicopter.

and on 29 November, headed to Charlestown and the Boston Naval Shipyard for a yard period that began on 3 December and ended 27 January 1972.

Until 15 March 1972, the carrier engaged in training and fleet exercises, following which she participated in Solid Oak, a combined exercise with Spanish and Portuguese naval units before a port visit to Rota, Spain, at the end of the month. In April she participated in another combined exercise with the Portuguese navy and making a port call in Lisbon in mid-April. Returning to Quonset Point on 23 April, she began working up off Narragansett and conducted a dependents day cruise on 15 June, giving an opportunity for the families of her crew to experience what it is like to be underway at sea on board a warship. On 1 July, she departed for her next deployment in the North Atlantic, with stops in Copenhagen, Denmark; Bergen, Norway; Rotterdam, Netherlands; Portsmouth, England; and Greenock, Scotland. She also participated in exercises Strong Express and Escort Deep before departing for Quonset Point. She arrived back in her home port on 20 October 1972.

On 24 November 1972, the *Intrepid* headed back across the Atlantic to relieve the *Franklin D. Roosevelt* in the Mediterranean. There she conducted exercises and made stops in Spain and Italy before the year ended. On 22 December 1972, while moored at Palma, Majorca, Captain Raymond H. Barker relieved Captain Williams. The carrier began 1973 in port at Naples before getting underway for refresher flight operations, followed by a port call at Cannes, France. In February she conducted ASW and strike exercises with NATO, which was a first for a carrier assigned to the Sixth Fleet. The exercises continued with the *Intrepid* making stops in Portugal, Spain, Italy, and Greece before returning to the United States on 25 April. During her last cruise to the Mediterranean, the *Intrepid* acted as a CV, developing and improving techniques for integration of attack and ASW aircraft. (The designations CV and CVN replaced CVA and CVAN on 30 June 1975 to reflect the multi-mission character of aircraft carriers after the decommissioning of the *Intrepid* as the last CVS in 1974. The *Hancock* and *Oriskany* had never been CVS carriers and continued to serve into 1976 as CVs.)

SUNSET

THE *INTREPID* WAS PLACED "IN COMMISSION IN RESERVE" ON 23 JULY
1973 as preparations began at Quonset Point for her mothballing. She
was the first carrier to complete the ship's force part of her inactivation
in her home port. The remaining crew, fewer than 700 men, spent
their time preserving their ship, dismantling shops and offices, and
refurbishing the equipment for use by other Atlantic Fleet ships and
shore facilities. Every vent, hatch, and port hole was sealed, and the
exterior was sandblasted to remove rust. A temporary sealer was also
put on the flight deck and the necessary preservation equipment and
materials were sent to the Philadelphia Naval Shipyard where the rest
of the preservation work would be completed. On 10 August 1973,
Commander Lee E. Levenson relieved Captain Barker and a few days

Intrepid being towed through the
lift bridge, gateway to the reserve
basin at the Philadelphia Naval Base,
where she was to be part of the
bicentennial exhibits from 4 July
1975 through 30 December 1976.

UNITED STATES NAVAL INSTITUTE

later, on the 16th, her crew took time out from their work to observe the *Intrepid*'s 30th birthday. On 15 March 1974, she was decommissioned and placed in the Reserve Fleet during a ceremony at Quonset Point.

After being nosed through a lift bridge, the *Intrepid* arrived at the Philadelphia Naval Shipyard. Over the next three months she completed her deactivation process. This included pumping dehumidified air throughout the ship to prevent rust. As the Official U.S. Navy and Marine Corps Bicentennial Exposition Vessel, she took part in the celebration of the Navy's 200th birthday on 13 October 1975 as well as the nation's bicentennial. Events included tours of aircraft, ship models, and other exhibits on the hangar deck, including multimedia presentations, dioramas, and displays showing propulsion systems from sail to nuclear power, submarine development, oceanography, historic Marine uniforms, and the Navy's part in space programs.

Several ideas to save aircraft carriers from scrapping had circulated for a number of years in the early 1970s. One idea put forth by a group called "Odysseys in Flight" was to build a short takeoff and landing port in New York City using two decommissioned aircraft carriers welded bow to bow. This effort eventually fell through, but one of the enthusiasts from this group, Michael Piccola, came up with the idea of an aircraft carrier museum with aircraft displayed

on the flight deck and began working on the necessary government paperwork to obtain an aircraft carrier from the Navy. An attempt to obtain the *Lexington* did not work out as she was still in commission at the time and committed to becoming a museum in Corpus

Crowds of visitors board the decommissioned *Intrepid* to view displays of aircraft, uniforms, ship models, motion pictures, and other exhibits of the Navy and Marine Corps Bicentennial Program, October 1975.

Military and civilian visitors tour the exhibits on the hangar deck of the *Intrepid* during the Philadelphia Naval Base Open House, October 1975.

Christi, Texas, which eventually opened in 1992. Larry Sowinski, author and historian, became part of the group in 1976, and through a network of different contacts met Zachary Fisher, a prominent New Yorker involved in construction and real estate. He would become a key figure in the effort to save the *Intrepid*.

Born in Brooklyn in 1910, Zachary Fisher left high school at age 16 to help his father and older brothers in the family construction business. His knee was severely injured in a construction accident, preventing him from serving in the military during World War II, but he made his contribution in other ways by helping the U.S. Army Corps of Engineers build coastal fortifications. The family business prospered, and after the war Fisher and his wife Elizabeth, who had been a USO entertainer, became active in work for wounded veterans. Fisher's reputation as a man who got things done and who remembered veterans led to an invitation to a meeting with prominent businessmen in November 1978. At the meeting Larry Sowinski told them of the *Intrepid*, which was scheduled to be scrapped. Later, Sowinski took Fisher to Philadelphia, where the *Intrepid* had been since the bicentennial. With his bad leg Fisher could not make it up the gangway, so Sowinski,

a large bear of a man, carried him up piggyback. The *Intrepid* was in sad shape from years of neglect. It was a daunting task, but Fisher was determined to save the ship. On 27 February 1979, the Intrepid Museum Foundation was created. The first step was to get the Navy to release the ship since an aircraft carrier had never been transferred to a private foundation before—the *Yorktown* museum that opened in 1975 had been released to the Patriot's Point Development Authority, which had been established by the state of South Carolina. The Navy sets stringent standards for donating a warship as a museum.

First, the organization that receives the ship must be a nonprofit corporation registered and approved by the state where the museum will be located. The organization must be properly organized with a corporate seal, by-laws, a charter registered by the state, and a tax-exempt number from the Internal Revenue Service, as well as other requirements, such as financial viability. The purchase of the *Intrepid* was financed by the sale of bonds and a loan from the city. Another challenge was the building codes for the City of New York, which did not consider the nature of a steel ship. Fortunately, Ed Koch, then-mayor of New York, considered the

Secretary of the Navy John F. Lehman Jr. signing the papers that transferred the decommissioned *Intrepid* for use as a museum in New York City, 27 April 1981.

Intrepid under tow just after passing under the Verrazano-Narrows Bridge on her way to Bayonne, New Jersey to be refitted as a museum in New York, 26 February 1982.

Intrepid project an important part of development for the West Side and saw to it that the building codes were modified and that Pier 86, where *Intrepid* was to be tied up and restored, was prepared. A federal loan obtained by the city provided additional funding. In February, the *Intrepid* was towed from Philadelphia to the Bethlehem Ship Yard in Hoboken, New Jersey, for restoration, which turned out to be more extensive and costly than originally planned. On 12 June Zachary and Elizabeth Fisher, accompanied by Larry Sowinski, boarded the *Intrepid* at Bayonne, New Jersey, for the six-and-a-half-hour journey to her new home in midtown Manhattan. After solving a number of problems, such as lack of electrical power and the installation of exhibits, the Intrepid Sea, Air & Space Museum opened to the public on 4 August 1982.

Because of the delays in opening, the attendance did not reach the expected levels that first year, but Zachary Fisher quietly kept paying the bills. Determined to keep the museum going, he renegotiated the loan from the city, sought donations from local businesses, and continued to pour in his own money. By 1985, attendance had picked up and in 1986 the *Intrepid* was designated a National Historic Landmark. The rededication of the Statue of Liberty that same year would also bring millions of visitors to New York and the *Intrepid* participated in the 100th birthday celebration of the statue, as well as the opening of the Jacob K. Javits Convention Center

in the area. The submarine *Growler* (SSG-557) was added to the museum in 1988 and the destroyer *Edson* (DD-439) the following year. (*Edson* later became a museum ship in Michigan and *Growler* was renovated in 2009.) During the attacks on the World Trade Center on 11 September 2001, the *Intrepid* served as temporary field headquarters for the Federal Bureau of Investigation as it began its investigation of the attacks.

A starboard quarter view of the docked *Intrepid* before being refitted as a museum, 26 February 1982.

After spending 24 years tied up to Pier 86, the *Intrepid* was closed to the public in October 2006 so that both the carrier and pier could undergo a $60 million restoration. In preparing for the move, dredges pumped 15,000 cubic tons of muck from the ship's path and 600 tons of water was pumped from her tanks. On the first

The *John F. Kennedy* (CV-67) (center) and the *Intrepid* flank various international naval vessels in New York City harbor during the International Naval Review 2000 (INR 2000), "Celebration of Sea Power for the Millennium," 5 July 2000.

attempt to move her on 6 November, one of her former skippers, retired Rear Admiral J. Lloyd "Doc" Abbot Jr. presided as news media provided live coverage of the event. After the mooring lines were ordered to be cast off, six tugs began easing her out. After moving only 15 feet, her propellers got stuck in the mud before she had even gotten out of her berth. After extensive dredging and removing her propellers, a second successful attempt was made on 5 December 2006. She was towed down the Hudson River to Bayonne to undergo restoration while the pier was being renovated. The aircraft carrier was later taken to Staten Island where her museum facilities were upgraded and expanded before returning

to her renovated pier in Manhattan, where she reopened on 8 November 2008 with more aircraft on display. A British Airways Concorde supersonic transport was also moved into an exhibit space on the pier. The museum continued to grow as the space shuttle *Enterprise* was added to her collection in 2011, requiring some aircraft to be transferred to the Empire State Aerosciences Museum near Schenectady, New York.

The Intrepid Sea, Air & Space Museum continues in its dedication to the exhibition and interpretation of history, science, and service through displays of historic aircraft, original artifacts, archival video footage, and interactive exhibits.

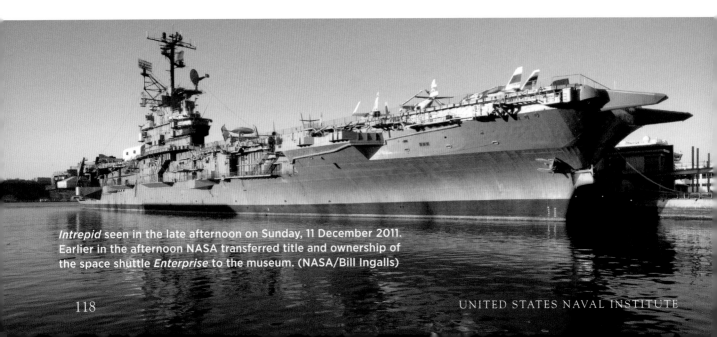

Intrepid seen in the late afternoon on Sunday, 11 December 2011. Earlier in the afternoon NASA transferred title and ownership of the space shuttle *Enterprise* to the museum. (NASA/Bill Ingalls)

Commanding Officers

Commissioned	**16 August 1943**
Captain Thomas L. Sprague	16 August 1943–28 March 1944
Captain Richard K. Gaines*	28 March 1944–19 April 1944
Captain William D. Sample	19 April 1944–19 May 1944
Captain Richard K. Gaines*	19 May 1944–30 May 1944
Captain Joseph F. Bolger	30 May 1944–15 February 1945
Captain Giles E. Short	15 February 1945–31 January 1946
Captain Robert E. Blick Jr.	31 January 1946–11 April 1946
Captain Henry G. Sanchez**	11 April 1946–4 November 1946
Commander Arthur A. Giesser	4 November 1946–22 March 1947
Decommissioned	**22 March 1947**
Recommissioned	**9 February 1952**
Captain Benjamin B. C. Lovett	9 February 1952–9 April 1952
Decommissioned	**9 April 1952**
Recommissioned in reserve	**18 June 1954**
Captain William T. Easton	18 June 1954–26 May 1955
Captain George L. Kohr	26 May 1955–15 August 1955
Captain Paul P. Blackburn Jr.	15 August 1955–21 September 1956
Captain Forsyth Massey	21 September 1956–4 October 1957
Captain Joseph H. Kuhl	4 October 1957–4 October 1958
Captain Paul Masterton	4 October 1958–30 August 1959
Captain Edward C. Outlaw	30 August 1959–8 September 1960
Captain Charles S. Minter, Jr.	8 September 1960–24 May 1961
Captain James L. Abbot Jr.	24 May 1961–14 June 1962
Captain Robert J. Morgan	14 June 1962–20 April 1963
Captain John C. Lawrence	20 April 1963–30 April 1964
Captain Joseph G. Smith	30 April 1964–13 May 1965
Captain Giuseppi Macri	13 May 1965–15 July 1966
Captain John W. Fair	15 July 1966–26 June 1967
Captain William J. McVey	26 June 1967–22 June 1968
Captain Vincent F. Kelley	22 June 1968–22 November 1968
Captain Whitney Wright***	22 November 1968–18 December 1968
Captain Vincent F. Kelley	18 December 1968–1 August 1969
Captain Horace N. Moore Jr.	1 August 1969–1 April 1970
Captain Isham W. Linder	1 April 1970–30 April 1971
Captain Charles S. Williams Jr.	30 April 1971–22 December 1972
Captain Raymond H. Barker	22 December 1972–10 August 1973
Commander Lee E. Levenson	10 August 1973–15 March 1974
Decommissioned	**15 March 1974**

* XO, Acting CO   ** With additional duty as XO   *** Acting CO

Awards

- Navy Unit Commendation (2)
- Navy Expeditionary Medal
- China Service Medal (extended)
- American Campaign Medal
- Asiatic-Pacific Campaign Medal (5 stars)
- World War II Victory Medal
- Navy Occupation Service Medal ("Asia" and "Europe" clasps)
- National Defense Service Medal
- Vietnam Service Medal (5 stars)
- Philippine Presidential Unit Citation
- Republic of Vietnam Meritorious Unit Citation (Gallantry Cross Medal with Palm)
- Philippine Liberation Medal
- Republic of Vietnam Campaign Medal
- Republic of Vietnam Meritorious Unit Citation (Gallantry Cross Medal with Palm)
- Philippine Liberation Medal
- Republic of Vietnam Campaign Medal
- During World War II *Intrepid* earned five battle stars:
  - One for the occupation of Kwajalein and Majuro (29 January–8 February 1944)
  - One for the Truk attacks (16–17 February 1944)
  - One for the capture and occupation of the Palaus and assaults on the Philippines (6 September–14 October and 9–24 September 1944)
  - One for Third Fleet supporting operations and attacks on Okinawa, Luzon, Formosa, and Visayas and the Battle of Leyte Gulf (10 October, 13–15 October, 17–19 October, 21 October, 24–26 October, 5–6 November, and 19–25 November).
  - One for Fifth and Third Fleet raids in support of Okinawa operations (17 March–16 April 1945)

Zachary and Elizabeth Fisher

Zachary Fisher was born in Brooklyn, New York, in 1910, the son of a Jewish Russian immigrant bricklayer. Fisher began working in construction at the age of 16, and in 1915 he founded Fisher Brothers with his brothers, Martin and Larry. Starting as contractors building homes outside Manhattan, the business grew into one of the real estate industry's largest residential and commercial developers. In 1942, after the attack on Pearl Harbor, he tried to join the Marines, but a leg injury due to a construction accident prevented him from serving in World War II. Despite this, he contributed to the war effort by assisting in the construction of coastal fortifications for the Army Corps of Engineers. In the 1970s, while still active in Fisher Brothers, he remained committed to both the Armed Forces and other philanthropic causes through his leadership role in a number of major projects. In 1982, he established the Zachary and Elizabeth M. Fisher Armed Services Foundation. Through the Foundation, he made significant contributions to the families of the victims of the bombing of the Marine barracks in Beirut in 1983. Since then, the Foundation has made major contributions to military families who have lost loved ones under tragic circumstances. Fisher's efforts to save the *Intrepid* began in 1978, leading to its becoming America's largest naval museum, which hosts nearly one million visitors annually. In 1990, Fisher and his wife, Elizabeth, established the Fisher House Foundation, which provides temporary lodging facilities for families at major military medical centers. (Elizabeth had served overseas with the United Services Organization in World War II, entertaining troops, volunteering for the Veterans Bedside Network, and visiting the wounded in field hospitals. They were married for 54 years before her death in 2004.) More than 70 Fisher Houses now operate at military bases and Department of Veterans Affairs medical centers across the nation. In 1994, in partnership with David Rockefeller, he established the Fisher Center for Alzheimer's Research Foundation, which funds research aimed at finding a cause and cure.

Fisher also supported the families of New York City firefighters who lost their lives in the line of duty. Throughout his life, Fisher held posts in a variety of charitable and arts organizations and military charities, serving as Honorary Chairman of the Board of Directors of the Marine Corps–Law Enforcement Foundation and supporting the Coast Guard Foundation, the Navy League, and other military charities. Fisher also established the annual Chairman of the Joint Chiefs of Staff Award for Excellence in Military Medicine. His support of artistic and cultural organizations included the Metropolitan Opera, Temple Israel, the Jewish Institute of National Security Affairs, the George C. Marshall Foundation, the Margaret Thatcher Foundation, the Reagan Presidential Library, the United Jewish Appeal, and many other organizations as well as serving on the boards of Carnegie Hall and several other institutions. The honors he has received include honorary doctorate degrees from the Massachusetts Maritime Academy and the Uniformed Services University of Health Sciences. In April 1995, Fisher was presented with the Presidential Citizens Medal by President Bill Clinton. In 1997, Fisher and his wife were given the Naval Heritage Award from the U.S. Navy Memorial Foundation for their efforts on the development of Fisher House. In 1998, Fisher received the Presidential Medal of Freedom from President Clinton in honor of his wide-ranging contributions on behalf of the young men and women in the U.S. Armed Forces. He also received the Horatio Alger Award, the Volunteer Action Award, the Senior Civilian Award from the Chairman of the Joint Chiefs of Staff and the Secretary of Defense, as well as the top awards a civilian can receive from each branch of the military. In 1995, Secretary of the Navy John Dalton announced that the second ship of the *Bob Hope* class of sealift ships would be named USNS *Fisher* (T-AKR 301) in honor of Zachary and Elizabeth Fisher for their commitment to improving the quality of life for our nation's sailors, Marines, airmen, and soldiers, saying, "There is no way to repay the Fishers for their decades of support, but this gesture, naming a ship in their honor—is the Navy's way of saying thank you very much." Before his death in 1999, the United States Senate introduced a bill that named Fisher as an honorary veteran of the Armed Forces. (Bob Hope is the only other person who shares the status of honorary veteran of the Armed Forces.)

Secretary of the Navy John F. Lehman Jr. (center) with *Intrepid* Museum Foundation president James R. Ean (left) look on as Zachary Fisher examines a model of the *Intrepid*, April 1981. Admiral Thomas B. Hayward, Chief of Naval Operations, stands in the background with Elizabeth Fisher.

On June 20, 1967, four pilots on board the aircraft carrier *Intrepid* steeled themselves for their first bombing mission over North Vietnam. The four bunkmates, who nicknamed their compartment "Triple Stix," expressed their mixed emotions in a shared diary. Forty years later, the pilots carefully packed the modest green logbook and donated it to their old ship.

The Triple Stix Log is just one of 20,000 items in the collection of the Intrepid Sea, Air & Space Museum. Entrusted to our care by former crew members and their families, these artifacts, archives, photographs, and oral histories speak to the diverse experiences and perspectives of *Intrepid*'s crew from 1943 to 1974.

Within *Intrepid*'s steel hull, 3,000 people from across the United States came together in service of their country. They drew upon Navy training that helped them work efficiently together, even under the duress of combat and individual fears. This shipboard community, like American society, was not without discord. Personal disputes, racial tensions, and even protests caused conflict among the crew. Our collections shine a light on the complexities of naval service in times of war, peace, and social change.

The Museum is committed to making our rich collections available to all. We invite you to explore the Museum's ever-growing digital collections at intrepid.emuseum.org. Discover the oral history of Eugene Smith, a World War II steward's mate who manned his gun in the face of a crash-diving enemy airplane. Explore the photographs of Robert Wayne Osburn, a photographer's mate whose striking compositions capture life and work on board an aircraft carrier at sea. Appreciate the artwork of Edward Ritter, whose cartoons captured the lighter side of life as a pilot.

While you are exploring, be sure to immerse yourself in the story of Triple Stix. In addition to the diary, the Museum's collections include oral histories, photographs, and artifacts from the pilots. Together, the Museum's collections capture the sweep of experiences on board an aircraft carrier at sea—from humor to boredom, to stress and grief.

Jessica Williams
Curator of History and Collections

ALL PHOTOS FROM THE COLLECTION OF THE INTREPID SEA, AIR & SPACE MUSEUM UNLESS OTHERWISE NOTED.

NATIONAL ARCHIVES

Six of the gunners who served in Gun Tub 10 on board *Intrepid*.

Four pilots from squadron VA-34, 1967.

OCT 10

    BERNIE ONLY GUY TO GET A HOP TODAY. WX REALLY BAD OVER BEACH. MAX Z'D FOR SOME MEMBERS OF TRIPLE STIXS.

OCT 11 - NO FLYING TODAY - SEVERA~~L~~ MANEXES, ~~NO LAUNCHES.~~

    TETER ~~RECEIVED WORD~~ ~~VI~~ RETURNE~~D~~ FROM VISITING THE ORISKANY WITH THE NEWS THAT DAVE HODGES WAS SHOT DOWN UP AT HANOI. A FEW DAYS AGO. GOT HIT BY A SAM. NO 'CHUTE SEEN. APARENTLY HE RODE IT IN.

Triple Stix Diary, 1967

UNITED STATES NAVAL INSTITUTE

OCT 12 — LAST DAY ON THE LINE
FOR THIS LINE PERIOD — 3 ALPHAS
SCHEDULED.

ONLY ONE ALPHA WENT — HAIPHONG —
BAD WX, 5/10 COVERAGE WITH BIG
CUMULUS BUILD UPS. THORNHILL GOT
HIT. LANDED ON THE SHIP OKAY —
4 HOLES IN ~~HIS~~ HIS LEFT WING — LOST
LOTS OF FUEL, ALSO BLEW A BIG
HOLE IN HIS CANOPY & BLEW THE
COVER OFF THE FACE CURTAIN HANDLE.
LUCKY GUY.

WE CAME IN FROM SE AND ORBITED
HAIPHONG TO THE NORTH DOING A 330°
CIRCLE TO ROLL-IN. THIS IS AN
UNPRECEDENTED MANUEVER AND WOULD
HAVE BEEN SUICIDAL IN THE PAST. NO
SAMS, LIGHT FLAK.

RUNNER LEFT FOR THAILAND.
ANY BETS ON HOW MANY F4 MISSIONS
HE FLYS?

GIFT OF NAVAL AVIATORS BEN HEALD, JIM VANLIERE, BRIAN WALKER & BERNARD FIPP

Collection of goggles

Uniform collection

World of Warships is a free-to-play, naval warfare–themed, massively multiplayer online game produced and published by Wargaming. Like their other games, World of Tanks (WoT) and World of Warplanes (WoWP), players take control of historic vehicles to battle others in player-versus-player or play ccooperatively against bots or in an advanced player-versus-environment (PvE) battle mode. World of Warships (WoWs) was originally released for PC in 2015; the PlayStation 4 and Xbox One console versions, titled World of Warships: Legends, followed in 2019, and it was released on the PlayStation 5 and Xbox Series X/S in April 2021.

Developed by Lesta Studios in St. Petersburg, Russia, World of Warships (PC) currently has more than 44 million registered players—playing on five main servers across the globe. More than 500 dedicated staff members work on a four-week update cycle to bring new features, ships, and mechanics to the game—keeping gameplay fresh and inviting to new players. The game features more than 400 ships, spread across 12 different in-game nations. Ships are designed based on historical documents and actual blueprints from the first half of the 20th century, and it takes from two to six man-months on average to create each of these ships. There are more than 20 ports to choose from, and 10 of them are re-created based on historical harbors and port towns.

There are four different ship classes: destroyers, cruisers, battleships, and aircraft carriers, with each class offering a different gameplay experience. Submarines have been in testing cycles since 2018, and based on testing results and player feedback, they have undergone significant changes that should allow them to launch as the fifth class in the near future. Ships are arranged in tiers between I and X, and players must progress through ship classes and tiers to reach tier X. Ships of tier X represent the pinnacle of naval engineering from World War II and the early Cold War era. Each warship needs a naval commander to lead it into the battle. There are many commanders to choose from in World of Warships, including more than 10 iconic historical figures. In World of Warships players can battle on more than 40 maps. There are seven different permanent or seasonal Battle Types to choose from: Co-op Battles, Random Battles, Ranked Battles, Clan Battles, Brawls, Scenarios, and Training. Additionally, within Battle Types there are four different Battle Modes available: Standard, Domination, Epicenter, and Arms Race.

Aircraft carriers are one of the four ship types that have been in World of Warships (PC) since the game's release. Their gameplay is based on the control of squadrons. A carrier's main goal is to strike at any location on the map, scout, and counter enemy aircraft. Originally, aircraft carriers in World of Warships had "strategic" gameplay: the player would send several of his squadrons on "battle missions" at once using a tactical map, without direct control of the planes. In update 0.8.0 (January 2019) the gameplay of this class was completely changed: now the player directly controls one squadron, evades explosions from AA, and directs flights into attack runs. The game currently features such U.S. aircraft carriers as Langley, Ranger, Lexington, Midway, Saipan, and others, while more will join in the future. World of Warships: Legends, in turn, currently features three nations that have aircraft carriers as part of their fleets: U.S., Japan, and Germany, with the American branch offering a chance to helm *Langley*, *Ranger*, and *Lexington*.

Developed by the team behind *World of Warships* for PC, *World of Warships: Legends* is a completely new entry in Wargaming's flagship nautical franchise that takes full advantage of the power and capabilities of home consoles. *World of Warships: Legends* brings the online naval action loved by millions to home consoles for the very first time, alongside a host of content and features exclusive to the console experience. *World of Warships: Legends* is now available for download from the PlayStation® Store and Microsoft Store. Players can now wage wars across a variety of maps, in numerous warships, and enjoy stunning oceanic vistas with glorious HDR support on PlayStation®4 and Xbox One X. Full 4K support is available on PlayStation®4 Pro, PlayStation®5, and Xbox One X too! *Legends* also supports standard high-def on PlayStation®4 and Xbox One, with more intriguing graphics on the horizon.

Wargaming preserves naval history by making a series of documentaries on museum ships. Since 2014, Wargaming Saint Petersburg published 50 episodes devoted to the world's most popular museum ships in the United States, Great Britain, Canada, France, Japan, Germany, Greece, Australia, Sweden, Poland, Russian Federation, and China. Documentary videos cover all main classes of warships engaged in world wars such as aircraft carriers, battleships, cruisers, destroyers, and submarines. If you are interested in learning about the birth and development of U.S. naval aviation, please scan the QR-code below with your cell phone or simply find the respective video on YouTube by typing its name: "Naval Legends: Birth and Development of US Naval Aviation."

The United States Naval Institute (USNI) has been a proud partner of *World of Warships* and Wargaming since December 2019. Wargaming has a made a commitment to naval history through various programs and events over the past years. It produces excellent video content with its *Naval Legends* series on YouTube, and hosts events on board museum ships where members of the gaming and naval history communities can get together and experience living history in person. *World of Warships* and Wargaming are also great sponsors of the Historic Naval Ships Association (HNSA). USNI thanks Wargaming and *World of Warships* for their continued support of the naval history community and their participation in this Naval History Special Edition. Please see the back cover for a special offer for *World of Warships* PC and *World of Warships: Legends*.

WORLD OF WARSHIPS

U.S. NAVAL AVIATION

⚓ NAVAL LEGENDS

USS *Intrepid*

UNITED STATES NAVAL INSTITUTE

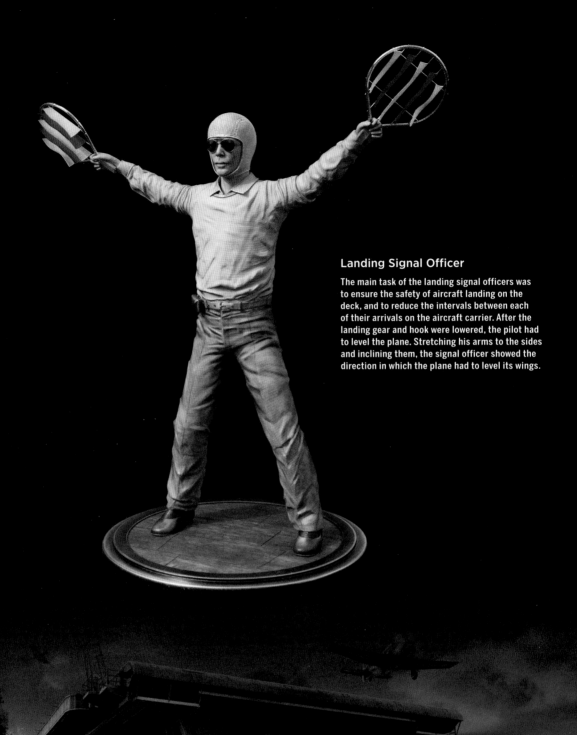

Landing Signal Officer

The main task of the landing signal officers was to ensure the safety of aircraft landing on the deck, and to reduce the intervals between each of their arrivals on the aircraft carrier. After the landing gear and hook were lowered, the pilot had to level the plane. Stretching his arms to the sides and inclining them, the signal officer showed the direction in which the plane had to level its wings.

USS *Essex*

UNITED STATES NAVAL INSTITUTE

Grumman TBF Avenger

The prototype of the carrier-based torpedo bomber TBF, developed by Grumman company, was first presented on 7 December 1941, the day of the Pearl Harbor attack. The order to start mass production of the new aircraft, immediately dubbed as the "Avenger," followed rather quickly. The plane that came off the assembly lines in the spring of 1942 was large and heavy, but this was its main advantage: due to the large volume of its fuel tanks, the aircraft had an unsurpassed action radius. Additionally, its capacious bomb compartment enabled it to carry a 570-mm torpedo or more than 900 kg of bombs. Moreover, the torpedo bomber was armed with machine guns, and the seats for its three crew members were well protected by armor. A powerful 1,900 hp engine ensured that this heavy load reached its destination, and at an excellent speed. From August 1942, every large-scale operation in the Pacific Theater involved Avengers. Their load capacity, range, and potential for refurbishment ensured that the Avengers had a long career in the armed forces of seven countries.

20-mm Oerlikon

In 1940, during the war, the United States began looking for a replacement for the obsolete and weak Browning AA machine guns. The 20-mm automatic Oerlikon, significantly improved by that time, proved to be very useful. In 1941, production began in the U.S., and soon the Oerlikons were mounted on almost every warship, from boats to battleships, and even aircraft carriers.

USS *Enterprise*

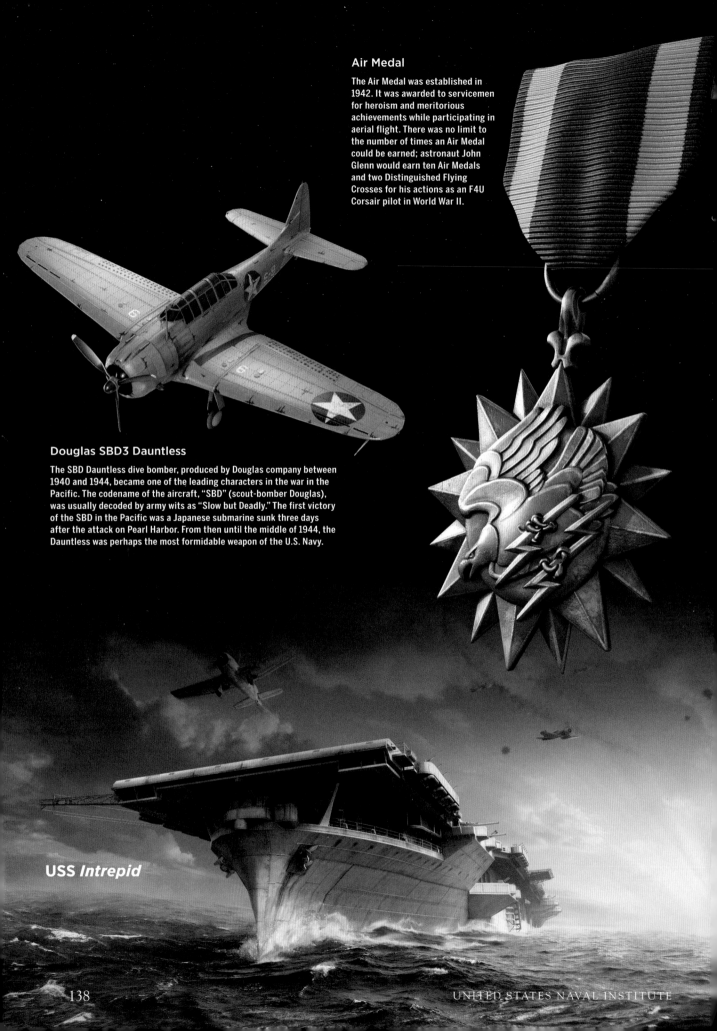

Air Medal

The Air Medal was established in 1942. It was awarded to servicemen for heroism and meritorious achievements while participating in aerial flight. There was no limit to the number of times an Air Medal could be earned; astronaut John Glenn would earn ten Air Medals and two Distinguished Flying Crosses for his actions as an F4U Corsair pilot in World War II.

Douglas SBD3 Dauntless

The SBD Dauntless dive bomber, produced by Douglas company between 1940 and 1944, became one of the leading characters in the war in the Pacific. The codename of the aircraft, "SBD" (scout-bomber Douglas), was usually decoded by army wits as "Slow but Deadly." The first victory of the SBD in the Pacific was a Japanese submarine sunk three days after the attack on Pearl Harbor. From then until the middle of 1944, the Dauntless was perhaps the most formidable weapon of the U.S. Navy.

USS Intrepid

UNITED STATES NAVAL INSTITUTE